Drafting and Negotiating Petroleum Royalty Agreements

Author
Peter Roberts

Managing director
Sian O'Neill

Drafting and Negotiating Petroleum Royalty Agreements
is published by

Globe Law and Business Ltd
3 Mylor Close
Horsell
Woking
Surrey GU21 4DD
United Kingdom
Tel: +44 20 3745 4770
www.globelawandbusiness.com

Printed and bound in Great Britain by Ashford Colour Press Ltd

Drafting and Negotiating Petroleum Royalty Agreements

ISBN 9781787427983
EPUB ISBN 9781787427990
Adobe PDF ISBN 9781787428003

DISCLAIMER
This publication is intended as a general guide only. The information and opinions which it contains are not intended to be a comprehensive study, or to provide legal or financial advice, and should not be treated as a substitute for legal advice concerning particular situations. Legal advice should always be sought before taking any action based on the information provided. The publishers bear no responsibility for any errors or omissions contained herein.

Index

Table of contents

Introduction

Petroleum royalty agreements are used extensively in relation to petroleum production in Australia, Canada and the United States (where, in each case, the form of the royalty agreement is localised and relatively formulaic, being related to the creation of an incorporeal real property interest).

Royalty agreements are increasingly being used in the petroleum sectors of South America, Africa, the Middle East, Eastern Europe, Central Asia and the Far East. In these regions, the royalty agreement takes the form of a contractual arrangement between the parties, which is often structured with little precedent or guidance in mind, and which will vary in complexity to reflect elements such as the size, the value and the duration of the intended transaction, and also the ambitions of the parties. Sometimes these royalty agreements will be ill-disciplined, poorly crafted documents which exhibit deficiencies in how they are worded; and they can depend for their effectiveness on the application of broad concepts and detailed drafting whose intention is best known only to the original authors. Because of this in-built opacity, some royalty agreements are accidents waiting to happen – and happen they will when there are later difficulties of interpretation between the parties where there is a dispute as to the intended meaning of the words which were used in the agreement.

This Special Report looks at how royalty interests in relation to petroleum production projects (and the wider royalty agreements in which such interests are represented) are (or could be) created, structured and applied. It consists of five parts, as follows:

- **Part A: Introduction to royalty interests** – the definition and form of a royalty interest, how royalty interests are characterised and how royalty interests are typically created in practice.
- **Part B: The economic underpinning of royalty interests** – the essential economic arrangements which underpin the principal forms of royalty interest.
- **Part C: Basic elements of a royalty agreement** – a consideration of the basic elements which are found in most royalty agreements.
- **Part D: Additional provisions in a royalty agreement** – a consideration of certain additional provisions which can be found in a royalty agreement.
- **Part E: Related arrangements** – a consideration of certain petroleum project arrangements which could entail the use of, or which could recite certain of the terms of, a royalty interest.

The drafting suggestions for the various terms of a royalty agreement which are set out in this Special Report represent the counsel of perfection. Rarely will a royalty agreement describe its essential legal and economic workings in the same level of detail as the suggested drafting; but it is better to see things the way they ought to be rather than the way they often are.

I am grateful for assistance given by Alice England, Sean Korney and David Sweeney. The responsibility for any errors is mine alone, of course.

The views expressed in this Special Report are my own and are neither representative of, nor attributable to, any entity with which I am or have been associated.

Peter Roberts
June 2021

Part A: Introduction to royalty interests

This part considers the definition and form of a royalty interest, how royalty interests are characterised and how royalty interests are typically created in practice.

A1 The essential elements of a royalty interest

In broad terms, a 'royalty interest'[1] is an arrangement whereby a person (in this Special Report called 'the producer')[2] which is party to the concessionary interests (a term which is examined further in A4) grants to another person (in this Special Report called 'the royalty holder')[3] a defined share of the petroleum to which the producer is entitled under the concessionary interests.

Within this summary, the key elements to note are the definition of produced petroleum to which the royalty interest applies, the subject interest of the producer in the concessionary interests and the royalty rate. Each of these elements is examined further at A5, A6 and A7 respectively.

A royalty interest will be recited in a wider royalty agreement, which is entered into between the producer and the royalty holder. The royalty agreement is the framework which enables the royalty interest to function.

'Petroleum' – which, after all, is what the royalty interest is all about – should be defined in the royalty agreement. 'Petroleum' could mean any of, or any combination of, crude oil, natural gas or natural gas liquids; and could also relate to (or could distinguish between) conventional and unconventional resources. Whether or not the royalty agreement relates to non-petroleum minerals might also be spelled out. It may seem an obvious point, but a royalty agreement should be careful to define the petroleum fractions to which the royalty interest is intended – and is not intended – to apply (and whether the royalty interest will apply differently to different petroleum fractions).

A royalty interest could be represented by the producer making available to the royalty holder physical volumes of petroleum at a defined point (called a 'royalty in kind'), or by payment by the producer to the royalty holder of a share of the proceeds of sale of the producer's petroleum entitlements (called a 'cash royalty'). These constructions are examined further in Part B.

There is no standard or generally accepted form of a royalty interest, or of a royalty agreement. Several popular descriptions of a royalty interest are referenced in this Special Report, but these descriptions are not terms of art which have universally accepted meanings. The international petroleum industry has not sought to settle the terms of a standard model form royalty agreement which is intended for international, regional or domestic application in the same way as it has for most other petroleum project agreements.[4] Consequently, a royalty agreement should be written carefully to reflect the required commercial intention of the parties, with the substance of the arrangement having more importance than whatever the form of the arrangement is professed to be.

A2 The characterisation of a royalty interest

A 'royalty interest' is essentially an economic arrangement which reflects the grant by the producer of a defined interest in produced petroleum (whether in kind or in cash) to the royalty holder, without a transfer by the producer to the royalty holder of a formal interest in the concessionary interests which underlie the production of petroleum (although this point is not always so (C1)), without giving the royalty holder rights to interfere in the day-to-day management of the concessionary interests, and without giving the royalty holder a formal security interest over the concessionary interests or a right of recourse to the wider assets of the producer in order to realise its expectations under the royalty interest. This last point means that a royalty interest should not offend any negative pledge covenants to which the producer is subject and should not require a royalty interest to be prioritised within the producer's wider debt portfolio (although

"There is no standard or generally accepted form of a royalty interest, or of a royalty agreement. Several popular descriptions of a royalty interest are referenced in this Special Report, but these descriptions are not terms of art which have universally accepted meanings."

the producer's lenders could demand the right to approve, or at least to be notified of, the producer's creation of a royalty interest).

A royalty interest will reflect the commercial intentions of the producer and the royalty holder; and each will have a certain impression as to the content, the effect and the character of that interest. There could, however, be circumstances in which a taxation authority or a regulatory agency chooses to take a different view of the nature of the royalty interest. This could expose the producer and/or the royalty holder to the consequences of an alternative (and possibly undesirable) interpretation:

- **The royalty interest as a loan:** Where a royalty interest provides for the payment of a fixed payment to the royalty holder regardless of the performance of the concessionary interests, and/or the level of petroleum sales prices (B2) applies a step-in right in protection of the royalty holder's interests (D1) or allows for the prioritisation of the royalty interest over potentially competing interests (D7), an argument could be made that the royalty interest is more in the nature of a loan arrangement, with the producer as the borrower and the royalty holder as the lender. This could have accounting and taxation consequences which are different from those which the parties had intended.

Alternatively, a royalty interest could be consciously structured as a form of loan arrangement (A3.1).

- **The royalty interest as a controlling interest:** Rights which are given to the royalty holder through the ability to access operational information (C5), covenant protection (C8) and transfer controls (C13.1) could allow an argument to be made that the royalty holder is a *de facto* holder of the concessionary interests. This could expose the royalty holder to the risk of being included in the list of persons which might prospectively be made liable for the costs of decommissioning the infrastructure used in the production of petroleum.[5] Taking this even further, certain greenhouse gas (GHG) emissions reporting conventions suggest that a producer should account for 100% of the GHG emissions from an asset over which the producer has control, where the test of control could be defined in financial or in operational terms.[6]

A statement in the royalty agreement that the relationship between the parties does not create a joint venture or partnership arrangement between them, or that the royalty holder is not a lender and has only an economic and not a controlling interest, could be reliable only up to a point. The substance of the arrangement between the parties will be more important than the ostensible form of that arrangement. The producer cannot limit the ambitions of taxation authorities or regulatory agencies to widen their reach, and cannot offer an effective guarantee of immunity to the royalty holder against such a possibility.

Legal advice, related to the jurisdiction in which the concessionary interests are located and the governing law which is selected to apply to the royalty agreement (C6.1), should be taken to ensure that the royalty agreement is structured in a way which eliminates (as far as possible) the risks of an alternative characterisation which could have adverse consequences for either or both of the parties.

A3 How a royalty interest comes into existence

There are several situations in which a royalty interest could come into existence, as follows.

A3.1 A royalty interest as a vehicle to facilitate a financial investment

A royalty interest could be put in place where an investor advances funds to a producer to enable the producer to meet the costs of development of the concessionary interests for which the producer is otherwise liable. The advanced funds (which could be advanced as a single upfront payment or piecemeal on a going-forward basis) could be closely controlled by the investor, to ensure that the producer uses them only to fund the intended development costs (unless the parties agree that the advanced funds can be used for any purpose by the producer, subject only to creating the royalty interest in order to secure the repayment of those funds):

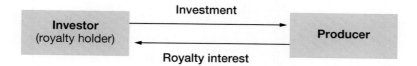

In this situation[7] the investor (as the royalty holder) would recover its investment over time through the payment of royalty amounts by the producer.

This construction is a form of synthetic farmout arrangement, which mimics the economic consequences of a farmout by the producer, but without applying the associated structural changes to the concessionary interests which a farmout arrangement would entail. It allows the producer to raise finance without diluting the producer's share of the concessionary interests and without affecting the degree of control which the producer has under those interests which would ordinarily follow under a farmout arrangement; and it allows the investor to participate in the fruits of the concessionary interests as a royalty holder, but (ordinarily) without being exposed to the risks which are associated with being a direct holder of those interests.

In this construction, the royalty interest could be represented as part of a wider loan arrangement, where the payments to be made to the royalty holder represent the gradual repayment of the amounts (as capital and with interest) which the royalty holder (as the investor) advanced to the producer.[8]

The financing of the development costs of a petroleum project by the use of a royalty interest is an alternative to a conventional debt financing (including reserves-based lending) or equity financing and offers several relative advantages:

- Accounting treatment: The royalty interest can be structured so that the obligation does not have to be accounted for as debt in the producer's books (although care needs to be taken in how the royalty interest is structured so that it does not contain commercial terms in favour of the royalty holder which would more readily suggest that it is a debt instrument). This means that the royalty interest can be created to secure additional funding without worsening the producer's debt position, gearing and debt covenant ratios.
- Quasi-equity characteristics: From the producer's perspective, the royalty interest is akin to the creation of an equity interest,

in that it allows third-party capital to be invested into the producer's business; but it does not entail the dilution of existing equity interests and neither does it reflect the element of control over the producer's business which might otherwise characterise a true equity interest.

- Cost of capital: In the producer's capital structure the obligation to make payments under the royalty interest typically ranks after debt commitments and ahead of equity commitments (unless the royalty interest is afforded particular protection in the management of competing interests (D7)). Consequently, the cost of capital which is associated with the royalty interest could be cheaper than the cost of equity, in exchange for an instrument which has many of the characteristics of an equity interest (see above).
- Reduced covenants: The covenants which are imposed on the producer by the royalty holder in the royalty agreement are typically less intrusive than the more extensive covenants which will exist to protect the lender's interests in a conventional debt instrument, and could apply less constraint on the producer (unless more extensive production covenants are negotiated to apply (C8)). Such covenants as there are in the royalty agreement could be limited to audit and verification rights (C2) and information rights (C5) in favour of the royalty holder, which are essential to protect the royalty holder's basic expectations.

"The covenants which are imposed on the producer by the royalty holder in the royalty agreement are typically less intrusive than the more extensive covenants which will exist to protect the lender's interests in a conventional debt instrument."

A3.2 A royalty interest as part of the sale consideration on a transfer of interests

A royalty interest could be put in place where an outgoing producer sells its share of the concessionary interests and takes a royalty interest (as the royalty holder) from the buyer (as the incoming producer) in respect of the concessionary interests which it has sold:

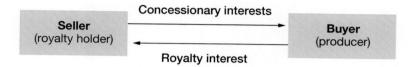

The royalty interest could represent the entirety or only a part of the consideration for the sale of the outgoing producer's interests which is payable by the buyer. The payment of royalty amounts to the outgoing producer (as the royalty holder) as part of the sale consideration represents a deferral of part of the price which would otherwise have been payable as an upfront amount on completion of the sale and purchase transaction by the buyer, thereby conferring a cash-flow benefit upon the buyer; and it could also (depending on the tax rules of the relevant jurisdiction) let the outgoing producer reduce the size of the potential capital gains charge tax which might otherwise apply on a disposal of its interests.[9]

A related situation to consider which sometimes occurs is where the producer sells a part only of its share in the concessionary interests to a buyer and takes a royalty interest in respect of the part of the concessionary interests which it has sold. In this circumstance, the seller (as the royalty holder) will also remain as a producer in respect of the concessionary interests. This could suggest the possibility of dispensing with a number of potential provisions in the royalty agreement (eg, the provision of operational information from the concessionary interests to the royalty holder (C5), and an indemnity in favour of the royalty holder against production-related liabilities (C9)). On the other hand, these royalty holder-friendly provisions might still be required in the royalty agreement, to address the possible future position where the producer sells its remaining share in the concessionary interests and becomes exclusively a royalty holder.

A3.3 The US model for petroleum exploitation

In the United States, it is common that a private landowner will also own the mineral interest resources which underlie its land (a concept known as 'ownership in place'). A common device to facilitate petroleum exploitation is for the landowner (as the lessor) to grant a lease to a petroleum exploration company to develop the resources (at the company's own risk and expense). In exchange for the grant of the lease the company (as the lessee) will, within the lease, grant a royalty interest to the landowner. The amounts payable by the company under the royalty interest are effectively part of the rental payments which are due to the lessor under the lease.[10]

Under the lease, it is commonly the case that the lessor will not be exposed to any of the costs and expenses which are associated with exploring for or producing petroleum. The lessee will be entitled to keep all the produced petroleum, after payment of the agreed royalty amounts (and other lease amounts) to the lessor.

To finance the costs and expenses which are associated with producing petroleum, the lessee could secure a financial investment from a third party and could grant a further royalty interest to that third party (where the third party would not be exposed to any of the costs and expenses which are associated with producing petroleum). Such a further royalty interest could also be granted by the lessee to various other third parties which have assisted the lessee in securing and developing the lease.

The common vernacular here is to describe:

- the landowner (ie, the lessor) as a 'royalty interest owner';
- the lease as a 'working interest';
- the company (ie, the lessee) as a 'working interest owner';
- a third party which has a further royalty interest as an 'overriding royalty interest holder'; and
- the working interest owner's share of the produced petroleum which it enjoys after the satisfaction of all of the operating expenses and royalty payments (to the lessee and to third parties) as the 'net revenue interest':

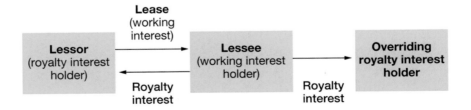

A particular feature of US royalty interests is how the lease and royalty arrangement between the lessor and the lessee will be subject to a number of implied covenants which will shape the rights and obligations relating to the royalty interest.[11] This means that the written words of the royalty interest within the lease might not necessarily be conclusive between them. This has frequently led to litigation and the generation of a significant body of jurisprudence relating to the definition of US royalty interests.[12]

In all three of the above situations, because the royalty holder's returns under the royalty interest are dependent on the production of petroleum from the concessionary interests, the royalty interest is of value to the royalty holder only where the concessionary interests are already producing petroleum or where they are near to producing petroleum. The royalty holder could commission a petroleum reserves report from an independent third party as part of a process of due diligence into the long-term prospectivity of the concessionary interests before entering into the royalty agreement. This requirement could be less imperative in the second situation, however, where the outgoing producer could already have adequate knowledge about the prospectivity of the concessionary interests which it is selling.

A4 The concessionary interests

A royalty agreement will typically make reference to the concessionary interests which govern the producer's entitlement to produce, lift and dispose of petroleum. The concessionary interests will be particularly relevant where the royalty interest takes the form of a real property interest (C1), and they could also be the subject of certain covenants under the royalty agreement (C8).

At the heart of the definition of the concessionary interests is the upstream petroleum granting instrument which is granted by the state to the producer for petroleum exploration and/or production (which could take the form of a licence, a production sharing contract, a revenue sharing contract or any other form of instrument), closely followed by the joint operating agreement (JOA) where the upstream petroleum granting instrument is held by multiple persons.

The definition of the concessionary interests could also reference other key petroleum project contracts and arrangements such as pooling or unitisation arrangements, transportation arrangements and other licences, permits and consents which are necessary to facilitate the production of petroleum:

Concessionary Interests means the Concession, the JOA and [identify other relevant agreements and accords].

Concession means the [identify the concession form] *for the exploration for and the production of* [Crude Oil] [Natural Gas] *from within the Concession Area to which the Producer is party dated* [insert the date] *and granted by* [identify the grantor].

Concession Area means the area which is granted in and which is defined by the Concession for the exploration for and the production of [Crude Oil] [Natural Gas].

JOA means the joint operating agreement in respect of the Concession to which the Producer is party dated [insert the date].

The concessionary interests could also undergo some redefinition through the application of a pooling or unitisation exercise (D8).

The royalty agreement should make clear whether the definition of the concessionary interests will include any additional interests which are subsequently acquired by the producer and which could otherwise be consolidated within that definition. Such an inclusion would not necessarily increase the subject interest (A6) or the royalty rate (A7) which applies to the royalty interest, but it would reflect a greater resource base to which the royalty interest would apply. The definition of the concessionary interests in the royalty agreement could also identify and exclude any other proximate concessionary interests to which the producer is party, which would be helpful to avoid the implication of the risks of conflict and consolidation (C3.2, C3.3) and to provide for rateable curtailment (D7).

It is possible that a single royalty agreement could be expressed to apply to more than one set of concessionary interests (and those interests might not be contiguous, or in any way related). This construction could apply from the outset of the royalty agreement or through the later addition of further concessionary interests. A separation of royalty interests by reference to specific concessionary interests is preferable in the interests of good estate management (C3.2, C3.3), including allowing a transfer of the royalty agreement with a transfer of the corresponding concessionary interests (C13).

The drafting examples in this section assume that the royalty interest will apply in respect of petroleum which is produced from the entirety of the concessionary interests, but it could be that the royalty interest will apply only in respect of defined, discrete development areas within a wider concession area; or the royalty interest could even apply on a well-by-well basis (a formulation which is suggested by the Canadian Association of Professional Landmen overriding royalty procedure (A2)). Where the royalty interest is applied to less than the entirety of the concessionary interests, the effective identification and the ring-fencing of the relevant petroleum quantities, costs and revenues will be essential.

The physical location at which the royalty holder's entitlement is determined should be defined in the royalty agreement. This 'delivery point' could be defined as the wellhead at the production facilities at which production is made available by the JOA operator to the parties to the JOA[13] and so to the royalty holder (where the delivery point could also be referenced as the fiscal metering point for produced petroleum at the wellhead):

"Whether the royalty holder's entitlement arises at the wellhead or at a further delivery point, the royalty agreement should provide that the royalty holder is subject to an obligation to lift the petroleum quantities to which it is entitled."

Delivery Point *means the wellhead at which the flow of Petroleum which is produced under the Concession is controlled* [and specifically means the point of fiscal metering of Petroleum at the wellhead].

Alternatively, the point of delivery of petroleum to the royalty holder could be a further point (which could also be the fiscal metering point for produced petroleum), in respect of which arrangements could need to be made for the transportation of petroleum from the wellhead to that further point (and in respect of which the allocation between the parties of the costs of such transportation could be an issue (B4)).

Whether the royalty holder's entitlement arises at the wellhead or at a further delivery point, the royalty agreement should provide that the royalty holder is subject to an obligation to lift the petroleum quantities to which it is entitled. This will also set up the conditions for the royalty holder's performance and breach of the royalty agreement (C7) and the possibility of *force majeure* relief (D5).

A5 The produced petroleum

The royalty interest will be determined by reference to the quantity of petroleum which is produced under the defined concessionary interests (A4) and made available to the producer. Consequently, the royalty interest will ordinarily have no application in respect of un-produced petroleum.

An essential function of the JOA is to establish the producer's lifting entitlement. This is the producer's share (which is determined by the producer's percentage participating interest under the JOA) of the total quantity of petroleum which is produced and made available by the JOA operator for lifting by the JOA parties in respect of a particular period of time.

The manner in which the producer's lifting entitlement is determined by the JOA should make it clear that the quantity of petroleum to which the royalty interest (in whatever form it takes (A1)) applies is net of any petroleum quantities which are lost, consumed or applied during the production process, and which are therefore not made available to the producer;[14] and is also net of certain operational and regulatory petroleum deductions (including royalties payable under the upstream petroleum granting instrument (B5)) which first must be accounted for by the JOA operator. This could be amplified in the royalty agreement by careful definition of the produced petroleum to which the royalty interest applies and does not apply (in this case, by reference to a royalty in kind – the comparable position for a cash royalty is considered in B2):

> *Produced Petroleum means in respect of a month the Producer's entitlement to any quantity of [Crude Oil] [Natural Gas] which is produced from the Concession Area, multiplied by the Subject Interest, which measure:*
>
> *(i) includes any quantities of [Crude Oil] [Natural Gas] produced under joint operations or under exclusive operations which the Producer has an interest in (including where such [Crude Oil] [Natural Gas] is produced from well workovers, recompletions, sidetracking, enhanced recovery or capture);*
>
> *(ii) excludes any quantities of [Crude Oil] [Natural Gas] which have been recovered by the Producer as payment in kind in lieu of monetary payments which are otherwise due to the Producer from the Producer's coventurers under the JOA;[15]*
>
> *(iii) excludes any quantities of [Crude Oil] [Natural Gas] which the Producer has no entitlement to because of the Producer's exercise of an election not to participate in an exclusive operation under the JOA;[16]*
>
> *(iv) excludes any quantities of [Crude Oil] [Natural Gas] which are*

reasonably and necessarily consumed and/or lost in drilling, processing or production activities in the Concession Area in connection with Production; and

(v) excludes any quantities of [Crude Oil] [Natural Gas] *which are payable as royalty in kind to the Government under the terms of the Concession.*

Government *means the lawful government of* [identify the jurisdiction] *and any agency or subdivision thereof.*

Production *means the production of Produced Petroleum.*

A6 The subject interest

The subject interest[17] is at the heart of the definition of the producer's obligation in respect of the royalty interest, since it determines the producer's share of the concessionary interests to which the royalty interest relates.

The subject interest could be defined by reference to the JOA:

Subject Interest *means, in respect of the Producer, the percentage participating interest which the Producer holds from time to time under the JOA.*[18]

Because of the reference back to the producer's participating interest under the JOA, the royalty amount which is payable could increase or decrease as the producer's participating percentage interest under the JOA increases or decreases over time. The royalty amount payable would inevitably become zero where the producer divests its interests under the JOA entirely (which could always happen, unless this is subject to management by certain conditions to the transfer of interests which are agreed in the royalty holder's favour in the royalty agreement (C13.1)).

It is unlikely that the subject interest in the royalty agreement would always be fixed as the producer's original participating percentage interest under the JOA, or at a deemed fixed level, since this could create a lack of relativity between the producer's (variable) subject interest and the royalty holder's (fixed) royalty entitlement.

To obviate the risk to the royalty holder of a reduced return under the royalty agreement which would result from a reduction of the producer's participating percentage interest under the JOA, the royalty agreement could recognise that the applicable royalty rate was originally agreed between the parties in relative terms by reference to the producer's subject interest as it was at the time of entry by the parties into the royalty agreement, and that the royalty holder's entitlement should always be maintained at the same relative level despite subsequent modifications to the extent of the producer's subject interest.

As an example to illustrate this, with the royalty holder having an initial royalty rate of 5% and the producer having an initial subject interest of 60%, the royalty holder would expect to receive three units of produced petroleum out of every gross 100 units of petroleum which are produced from the concessionary interests:

Total petroleum production from the concessionary interests	100 units
Producer's subject interest @ 60%	60 units
Royalty rate @ 5%	3 units
Producer's net take	57 units

If the producer's subject interest were subsequently reduced (whether by a partial transfer of the producer's interests (C13.1) or by application to a replacement upstream petroleum granting instrument (D11)), the relativity of the royalty holder's return could be maintained by increasing the royalty rate according to a formula where a fraction (the numerator of which is the original subject interest and the denominator of which is the reduced subject interest) is multiplied by the original royalty rate and which is then expressed as a percentage of 100. Continuing the above example:

Total petroleum production from the concessionary interests	100 units
Producer's subject interest @ 40%	40 units
Royalty rate @ 7.5%	3 units
Producer's net take	37 units

Such a mechanism in the royalty agreement should also provide that if the producer's subject interest is subsequently increased, then the relativity of the royalty holder's return will be adjusted proportionately (thereby resulting in a reduced royalty rate to reflect an increased subject interest). Both of the above adjustments would be effected by the following formula:

If at any time the Subject Interest is modified the Royalty Rate will be modified and will thereafter apply according to the following formula:

$$RRR = SI/RSI \times ORR \times 100$$

where:

RRR means the revised Royalty Rate which will apply after the application of this clause x

SI means the Subject Interest as it was prior to its modification

RSI means the Subject Interest as it is after its modification

ORR means the percentage of the Royalty Rate as it was prior to the application of this clause x

A7 The royalty rate

A royalty interest will recite the 'royalty rate', which will be the percentage share of the producer's petroleum entitlements to which the royalty holder is entitled under the royalty agreement.

Different royalty rates could apply to different forms of petroleum in the same royalty agreement (A1), or to varying volumes of produced petroleum on a sliding scale (B1), or during different phases of a royalty agreement (an example of this is where a royalty interest forms part of a payout arrangement (E2)).

The royalty rate which applies in the royalty interest will be the product of a negotiation between the producer and the royalty holder, to be determined as part of a wider package which reflects other factors such as the producer's subject interest (A6), general commercial factors which are negotiated to apply in the royalty agreement (A8), and the deductibility of costs and expenses under certain forms of cash royalty (B4).

As a starting point, the royalty rate could appear as a flat percentage:

Royalty Rate means 10% [of the Produced Petroleum] [of the proceeds of sale of the Produced Petroleum].

For onshore petroleum deposits in the United States, it is common to see the royalty rate based upon a one-eighth interest (ie, one-eighth (or 12.5%) of the produced petroleum or its value). The basis for such a subdivision is drawn from the US practice of dividing a single tract of land into eight eighths (ie, 8 × 12.5% interests).[19]

Some royalty agreements demonstrate an affinity for mixing up vulgar fractions and percentages in the definition of the royalty rate. It is not uncommon to find a royalty rate defined as "a five-eighths of three per cent royalty interest" (where the net position of $5/8 \times 3\% = 1.875\%$), or "a three per cent of eight-eighths royalty interest" (where the net position of $3\% \times 8/8 = 3\%$). Such a combined fractional and percentage interest as a method of expressing a royalty rate could start off this way in a royalty agreement, or it could be the result of a royalty interest which has been subdivided into eighths and then sold out in parts over time by the royalty holder (C13.2).

A8 The economic balance of the royalty interest
A royalty interest represents a commercial arrangement between the producer and the royalty holder which reflects an agreed balance of risk and reward. At the heart of that arrangement is the royalty holder's receivable, which is determined (in kind or in cash) by reference to a combination of factors: the producer's subject interest (A6); the royalty rate (A7); anticipated rates of petroleum production; and the duration of the royalty interest (C4.2).

In relation to a royalty interest, a number of commercial and operational risks inevitably exist, which apply for the duration of the royalty interest and which could adversely impact the royalty holder's expectations. Principally, these risks relate to:

"A royalty interest represents a commercial arrangement between the producer and the royalty holder which reflects an agreed balance of risk and reward."

- reserves risk (that the estimated petroleum resources in the producer's subject interest will be adequate);
- production risk (that the producer's subject interest will move into production petroleum and will sustain such production at target rates);
- market risk (that the produced petroleum will be a saleable commodity at adequate prices);
- business risk (that the producer (or even the producer's coventurers) will remain solvent and fully functioning); and
- general above-ground risks (that the concessionary interests will not be forfeited or exposed to adverse interference).

These are all risks to which the producer is also exposed, and so in these respects the producer and the royalty holder have a common exposure.

The interests of the producer and the royalty holder in relation to a royalty interest are ostensibly aligned because they should both benefit from the production of petroleum under the concessionary interests at the greatest possible rates of production (and for the longest possible periods of time), and from the sale of that petroleum at the highest possible prices (in the case of a cash royalty). Consistent with that, the producer and the royalty holder will both suffer from a failure of the concessionary interests (where the risk to the royalty holder is the failure to realise its expected returns from the royalty interest).

This alignment of interests is true only up to a point, however. If a royalty interest guarantees a minimum level of return to the royalty holder regardless of the performance of the concessionary interests and/or of the level of petroleum sales prices (B2, B3), including where the producer has procured some form of collateral support for the royalty holder for that minimum payment (D1), then the alignment of interests becomes less obvious because the royalty holder has secured a degree of insulation from the risk of a performance or market failure relating to the concessionary interests which the producer will not enjoy.

The royalty holder could require the inclusion of certain provisions in the royalty agreement which could de-risk the commercial proposition of the royalty interest from its perspective. These provisions could include:

- upward modulation of the royalty rate to track downward subject interest changes (A6);
- involvement in the producer's petroleum sales arrangements (B2);
- floor price and hedging protection rights in a net profit interest (NPI) (B2);
- the application of the royalty interest against the producer's successors and assigns (C1);

- rights to audit the producer's business (C2);
- rights to terminate the royalty agreement with a termination payment (C4.3);
- obligations of the producer to provide information (C5);
- ongoing production covenants given by the producer (C8);
- indemnities against production-related liabilities given by the producer (C9);
- control of the producer's ability to transfer its interests (C13.1);
- the application of a pre-emption right to a producer's transfer of its interests (C13.1);
- freedom to subdivide and transfer its interests (C13.2);
- the application of a redemption right in respect of the royalty holder's interests (C13.2, D9);
- warranties given by the producer (C14);
- the procurement of collateral support in respect of the producer's obligations (D1);
- the ability to convert the royalty interest to a concessionary interest (D2);
- protection of the royalty holder's interests against expropriation of the concessionary interests (D3);
- the right to participate in insurance recoveries (D6);
- the preference of the royalty interest over potentially competing interests (D7);
- protection of the royalty interest in the event of a pooling or unitisation of the concessionary interests (D8);
- the application of the royalty interest to replacement upstream petroleum granting interests (D11); and
- protection against negative royalty risks under an NPI (D12).

Correspondingly, the producer could also require the inclusion of certain provisions in the royalty agreement which could de-risk the commercial proposition of the royalty interest from its perspective. These provisions could include:

- downward modulation of the royalty rate to track upward subject interest changes (A6);
- payment against revenue rights (B2);
- extensive deductible costs definition in an NPI (B4);
- the subordination of the royalty interest rights to the JOA position (C7, C10);
- the application of a redemption right to apply in respect of the royalty holder's interests (C13.2, D9);
- the exclusion of liability for implied fiduciary duties (D4);
- the ability to claim *force majeure* relief in respect of its obligations (D5); and
- the ability to suspend the performance of its obligations (D12).

"Care will need to be taken to ensure that, according to the governing law which is selected to apply to the royalty agreement, the royalty agreement represents a valid and enforceable agreement which is entered into between the producer and the royalty holder."

In the negotiation of the terms of the royalty interest, the producer could argue that there are no free options – the de-risking of the commercial proposition of the royalty interest from the royalty holder's perspective through the accommodation of the royalty holder's requirements will result in the assumption of an increased risk profile for the producer, and consequently there should be a reduction to the royalty rate which reflects the improvement of the royalty holder's position at the expense of the producer. Correspondingly, the royalty holder could make the same point when it insists that the accommodation of producer protections in the royalty agreement should result in the application of a higher royalty rate. Thus is established the basis for the negotiation of the royalty agreement.

A9 The form of execution of a royalty agreement

Care will need to be taken to ensure that, according to the governing law which is selected to apply to the royalty agreement (C6.1), the royalty agreement represents a valid and enforceable agreement which is entered into between the producer and the royalty holder. This is principally so where the royalty interest takes the form of a contractual arrangement, rather than the form of a real property interest which would have its own conditions relating to form and enforceability (C1).

Under English law, a royalty agreement could be executed as a simple contract (ie, as a contract signed under hand), where the consideration which moves from the royalty holder (as the promisee) to the producer (as the promisor) could be expressed to be whatever the royalty holder has done to earn the royalty interest (whether that is the advance of a financial investment to the producer, a purchase of the producer's concessionary interests or the grant of a lease). Alternatively, the royalty agreement could be executed as a deed (subject to compliance with the prescribed formalities for the valid execution of a deed). This would obviate the need to assess the adequacy of the consideration and could apply a more extensive limitation period for the bringing of claims by and between the parties in relation to the royalty agreement.

A10 Mineral interest royalties

This Special Report looks at royalty agreements insofar as they relate to the production of petroleum. Royalty agreements are also widely used in the mining (minerals and metals) industry, representing the right of a person to receive a percentage of either the in-kind products of a mining operation or of the proceeds of sale of those products. For comparative reference, the principal forms of mining interest royalty agreements (which are quite different from petroleum royalty agreements by name, although in certain areas the substance of the two schools of agreement will be similar) which are used are as follows:

- Net smelter return royalty: This gives the royalty holder a share of the revenues which are realised by a mine owner from a sale of the processed in-kind products of a mining operation, calculated subject to the deduction of certain of the associated costs of transporting the products to the processing point and of processing the products (in smelters – hence the name).
- Gross revenue royalty (or gross overriding royalty (GOR)): This gives the royalty holder a share of the revenues which are realised by a mine owner from a sale of the in-kind products of a mining operation, but without recognition of the associated costs of processing or transportation (although some costs could be recognised for deduction).
- Net profit interest royalty: This gives the royalty holder a share of the mine owner's realised operating profits, which are typically calculated after the mine owner has recovered its capital costs and certain costs associated with processing the products.

As will be seen in respect of petroleum royalty agreements, the substance of the arrangement will always be more meaningful than the nomenclature which is used, and in reality a particular mining interest royalty could be an amalgam of the above forms.

Part B: The economic underpinning of royalty interests

This part considers the essential economic arrangements which underpin the principal forms of royalty interest.

The first major distinction to note in the classification of royalty interests is that which exists between a royalty in kind and a cash royalty.

A royalty agreement could recite both of the royalty in kind and cash royalty options in favour of the royalty holder, subject to a requirement of the royalty holder to make an election as to which formulation it requires (in which case the royalty agreement would need to contain all the drafting for a royalty in kind and a cash royalty, to be applied according to whichever election the royalty holder makes). The royalty agreement could also permit the royalty holder to change the election which it has made from time to time.

The ability to make these elections could be of value to the royalty holder where, for example, the royalty holder starts off with a cash royalty but later elects to take a royalty in kind when the royalty holder has a physical need for petroleum for in-country purposes such as refining; or where the royalty holder has established a petroleum trading function and has built up its own petroleum marketing competencies, and believes it could do better than the producer in selling its petroleum entitlements.

B1 The royalty in kind

In principle, this should be the most straightforward form of royalty interest to document and to apply. Under the terms of the JOA, the producer is entitled to lift and dispose of a defined share of the total quantity of produced petroleum (A4), further distinguished between crude oil and natural gas for the following example, and a defined percentage of that share is provided to the royalty holder in kind by the producer. The royalty agreement could say little more than that really:

> *In respect of each month the Producer will deliver and the Royalty Holder is entitled to receive, take delivery of at and dispose of from the Delivery Point the following percentages of Produced Petroleum:*
>
> *(a) Crude Oil – 10%*
>
> *(b) Natural Gas – 10%*

Structurally, this would appear as follows:

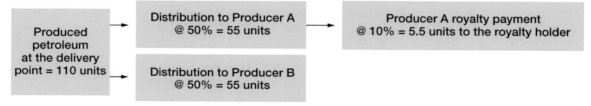

The concern of the royalty holder will be to ensure that the producer does all it can to maximise the rate of production of petroleum from the concessionary interests, and that the producer does so for as long as possible. The various mechanisms by which the royalty holder might be able to compel these objectives against a producer are considered in Parts C and D.

As a further refinement, a royalty agreement could apply a sliding scale to the definition of the royalty interest, with lower percentage royalty rates to apply as an offset to greater volumes of produced petroleum:

> *In respect of each month the Producer will deliver and the Royalty Holder is entitled to receive, take delivery of at and dispose of from the Delivery Point the following percentages of Produced Petroleum calculated by reference to the following rates (on the right).*

A royalty in kind gives the royalty holder a share of the produced petroleum to which the producer is entitled, which is typically made available to the royalty holder at the wellhead (A4) as the delivery

Produced petroleum per month		Royalty rate
Natural Gas – up to • million standard cubic feet (mscf)		10%
Natural Gas – • mscf to • mscf		9%
Natural Gas – greater than • mscf		8%
Crude Oil – up to • Barrels		10%
Crude Oil – • Barrels to • Barrels		9%
Crude Oil – greater than • Barrels		8%

point. To make the royalty holder's rights effective, the royalty agreement could recognise the necessary rights for the royalty holder to access the delivery point and to effect the removal of its in kind petroleum quantities, for transportation to a point of sale. Alternatively, the producer could carry out these functions for the royalty holder, subject to the royalty holder's commitment to pay the producer for the associated costs which are incurred in doing so.

The royalty holder will sell the petroleum which it receives from the producer in order to realise a monetary value. In the first instance, the producer could purchase the royalty holder's entitlements at the delivery point; but beyond that, the royalty holder could have no inclination for, and no means of, selling the petroleum which it is due to receive. The producer could therefore act as an agent for the sale of the royalty holder's entitlement (at market prices), and would account to the royalty holder for the sales proceeds.[20] The producer could charge an *ad valorem* marketing fee to the royalty holder for performing this sales agency function. Such agency sales would need to be managed carefully where there is a risk that the producer could sell the royalty holder's petroleum quantities to an affiliated or an associated person at an undervalue (B2).

B2 The cash royalty

Under a cash royalty, the producer sells its share of the total quantity of produced petroleum, and accounts to the royalty holder for a defined percentage of the resultant sale proceeds. The particular distinction to note in relation to cash royalties is between the following constructions:

- GOR:[21] The royalty interest is calculated as a defined percentage of the gross proceeds of sale of the produced petroleum which

Drafting and Negotiating Petroleum Royalty Agreements

are realised by the producer, without the deduction of any of the costs and expenses which were incurred by the producer in relation to producing that petroleum.

- NPI:[22] The royalty interest is calculated as a defined percentage of the proceeds of sale of the produced petroleum which are realised by the producer, after the deduction of certain of the costs and expenses which were incurred by the producer in relation to producing that petroleum.

A cash royalty could, depending on how it is drafted, fall anywhere in the range between the extremes of the two constructions which are described above. A royalty holder could hold a royalty interest which has the appearance of being a GOR, but which includes provision for the deduction by a producer of at least some of the associated production costs, so that the GOR starts to stray into the territory of being a form of NPI. Alternatively, a royalty holder could hold a royalty interest which is described as being an NPI, but which has a definition of deductible costs and expenses which is relatively restricted, so that the royalty interest is in practical terms closer to being a GOR. The actual substance of the royalty interest will always be more important than whatever its form is professed to be.

Despite making provision for the deduction of costs and expenses, it is not axiomatic that an NPI will be less valuable than a GOR to the royalty holder. An NPI which has a high royalty rate (A7) could, despite the deduction of costs and expenses, have a greater intrinsic value than a GOR with a lower royalty rate.[23]

Several refinements to the basic proposition of the GOR or the NPI could be made in the royalty agreement, as follows.

Payment against revenue: The royalty amount which is due for payment could be determined on the basis of the net sales proceeds which were actually received by the producer, rather than on the basis of the gross sales prices which were invoiced by the producer under the petroleum sales arrangements. This is sometimes represented by the phrase 'royalty based on receipts'. This would protect the producer against the risks of payment failure or the application of price adjustments (including permitted setoffs) which were associated with the sale of petroleum and which would impact the producer's expected revenues from the sale of the produced petroleum (C11).

Floor price protection: To protect the royalty holder from the risk of a reduction in revenue which is caused by falling market prices, the royalty agreement could apply a floor price for the sales of the produced petroleum (although the producer could understandably be reluctant to assume this risk):

Gross Values means: (i) for Crude Oil, the greater of: (a) the gross sales prices which were invoiced by the Producer for the sale of the Produced Petroleum (in US$ per Barrel); and (b) US$[•] per Barrel; and (ii) for Natural Gas, the greater of: (a) the gross sales prices which were invoiced by the Producer for the sale of the Produced Petroleum (in US$ per mscf); and (b) US$[•] per mscf.

Hedging protection: To protect the royalty holder from the risk of a reduction in revenue which is caused by falling market prices, the royalty agreement could provide that the petroleum will be sold under (and the royalty holder will benefit from) a hedging instrument which the producer has put in place:

If the Producer (whether itself or through an Affiliate) has at any time put in place or otherwise benefits from a Hedging Instrument then the amounts payable by the Producer to the Royalty Holder under clause x will be paid subject to and with the benefit of the Hedging Instrument in favour of the Royalty Holder where the application of the Hedging Instrument would result in payment to the Royalty Holder of an amount greater than the amount which would otherwise be payable to the Royalty Holder under clause x.

Hedging Instrument means any price hedge, commodity swap or other derivative instrument entered into in respect of the sale of Petroleum which is produced from the Concessionary Interests.

Undervalue petroleum sales: A risk to the royalty holder is that the producer could sell the produced petroleum to an affiliated or an associated person at a price which is an undervalue relative to true market prices in order to reduce the amount of royalty which is payable (with the affiliated or an associated person then on-selling that petroleum at true market prices), or that the producer could exchange petroleum for non-cash consideration in order to evade the royalty interest payment obligation altogether. To preclude these risks, the royalty agreement could provide as follows:

If the consideration which is received by the Producer for the Produced Petroleum is not cash (including any exchange of goods or services or any forbearance to sue), or if the Producer has (in the Royalty Holder's reasonable opinion) sold the Produced Petroleum to any person at an undervalue relative to objective market value, then the Gross Values will be deemed to be the Royalty Holder's assessment (acting reasonably) of the objective market value of the relevant Produced Petroleum, based upon the greatest sales price which a willing buyer would pay a willing seller in the open market based on arm's length contract terms.

The producer could be reluctant to accept the royalty holder's determination of what the market value should be in this situation, and the royalty agreement could instead apply an objective definition of the applicable market value.

Fixed price payment: What the royalty holder receives under each of the GOR and the NPI will vary according to realised petroleum sales prices. As a decoupling from price risk, the royalty agreement could provide for a fixed price payment to be made to the royalty holder, to be paid regardless of the level of the realised petroleum sales prices. This takes the royalty interest out of the realm of being an *ad valorem* interest, is essentially a hedging arrangement in favour of the royalty holder and means that the producer is taking the risk of realised petroleum sales prices falling below the fixed price payment level. If this provision is applied, the royalty agreement could also make provision for the periodic indexation and rebasing of the currency component in order to keep pace with inflation over time.

The economic exposure which a fixed price payment gives to the producer is obvious (which the producer could be willing to accept if the fixed price payment is set at a low enough level), and such an arrangement could contribute to the construction of the royalty interest as a *de facto* loan arrangement (A3.1). If this construction is adopted, the royalty agreement should be careful to structure the fixed price payment as a floor price which is payable under the royalty agreement, rather than as a standing amount which is payable in addition to any *ad valorem* royalty payment:

> *The Royalty Holder is entitled to receive and the Producer will pay to the Royalty Holder a guaranteed monthly amount in respect of Produced Petroleum calculated by multiplying each Barrel of Crude Oil which is produced by US$[•] and each mscf of Natural Gas which is produced by US$[•], which payment will be included as part of and offset against any amounts which are otherwise due for payment by the Producer to the Royalty Holder under clause x.*

Because the amount which the royalty holder will receive under a GOR or an NPI depends on the realised prices for the sale of petroleum, the royalty holder could have a particular interest in the terms of the petroleum sales arrangements which the producer enters into, and to this end the royalty holder could require provision in the royalty agreement that:

- the royalty holder can approve the identity of the buyer and the terms of the sales arrangements (which could include addressing matters such as limited payment deferral terms, the price and the management of price review terms, terminability, offsets and deductions, and the provision of collateral support by the buyer);

- the buyer could be required to make a part payment direct to the royalty holder, rather than payment being routed through the producer; and
- the royalty holder could have a right to enforce the terms of the sales arrangements directly against the buyer.

Whether the producer, or the buyer, would be at all willing to allow the royalty holder's involvement in the petroleum sales arrangements in such a manner is another matter.

The sales proceeds from the produced petroleum from which the royalty interest is derived would primarily be the price paid by the buyer under the petroleum sales arrangements, but could also include any take or pay payments which are made by the buyer. In the manner which was suggested in respect of certain quantities of petroleum which are excluded from being a royalty in kind (A5), the royalty agreement could make clear that the sales proceeds which are realised by the producer will not include certain other monetary income which is received by the producer under or in respect of the petroleum sales arrangements (eg, the receipt of insurance proceeds,

"The royalty agreement could make clear that the sales proceeds which are realised by the producer will not include certain other monetary income which is received by the producer under or in respect of the petroleum sales arrangements."

tax rebates, indemnity claims, monetary damages or the outcome of a dispute resolution process with the buyer). These elements might not obviously qualify as sales proceeds, but this might be a point worth making in the royalty agreement for absolute clarity.

B3 The gross overriding royalty

In this form of royalty interest, a defined percentage of the gross proceeds of sale of the producer's produced petroleum entitlements is provided to the royalty holder by the producer.

In the simplest case, the GOR could be calculated as the product of the gross revenues which result from the sale of petroleum, multiplied by the royalty rate:

> *In respect of each month the Royalty Holder is entitled to receive, and the Producer is obliged to pay, payment in cash in respect of the Produced Petroleum calculated by multiplying the Gross Values by the Royalty Rate.*
>
> ***Gross Values*** *means the gross sales prices which were invoiced by the Producer for the sale of the Produced Petroleum (in US$ per Barrel for Crude Oil and US$ per mscf for Natural Gas).*
>
> ***Royalty Rate*** *means 10%.*

Structurally, this would appear as follows:

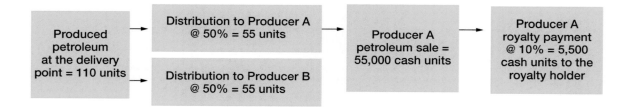

B4 The net profit interest

The apparent economic disadvantage of a GOR from the producer's perspective is that the incidence of the costs and expenses which are associated with the production of petroleum will fall exclusively on the producer.

To redress this, an NPI royalty interest provides, in broad terms, that the royalty amounts which are payable to the royalty holder will be determined as a percentage of the proceeds of sale of the produced petroleum which are realised by the producer, but after the deduction of certain of the costs and expenses which were incurred by the producer under the concessionary interests in relation to the production of that petroleum. This exposes the royalty holder to a share of the burden of the associated costs and expenses.[24] Relying only on such broad terms in order to define the royalty interest could be at the heart of a problem of interpretation of a royalty agreement, however.

The identification and the quantification of the deductible costs and expenses under an NPI could be represented in a royalty agreement by a formulation such as the following:

In respect of each month the Royalty Holder is entitled to receive, and the Producer is obliged to pay, the Net Profit Interest as a payment in cash in respect of the Produced Petroleum for the relevant month of calculation.

Net Profit Interest *means the Gross Values multiplied by the Royalty Rate, minus the Deductible Costs Share.*

Gross Values *means the gross sales prices which were invoiced by the Producer for the sale of the Produced Petroleum (in US$ per Barrel for Crude Oil and US$ per mscf for Natural Gas).*

Deductible Costs Share *means the Deductible Costs for which the Producer is liable for the relevant month of calculation, multiplied by the Royalty Rate.*

Royalty Rate *means 10%.*

Structurally, this would appear as follows:

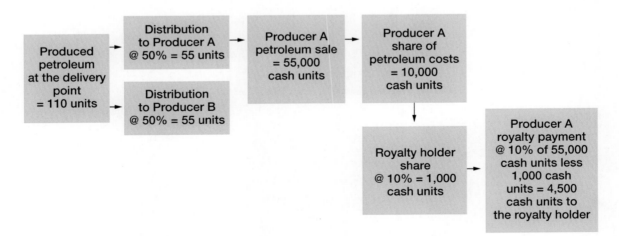

At the heart of the NPI is the definition of the costs and expenses (which are referred to as 'deductible costs' in this section) which are associated with the production of petroleum and which the producer is entitled to deduct from the sales proceeds, from which the royalty amount would then be derived. This is a key issue for debate in the negotiation of an NPI. The producer's interest is in making the definition of deductible costs as wide as possible in order to reduce the royalty amount which is payable, whereas a royalty holder has the opposite preference.[25]

As a starting point for negotiation, the deductible costs could be classified by reference to the following headings:

- Pre-production costs: Certain costs and expenses will be associated with the development of the concessionary interests before the production of petroleum begins. These 'pre-production costs' could include the costs and expenses of:
  - acquiring the upstream petroleum granting instrument;
  - exploration and appraisal seismic works and drilling;
  - production well completions; and
  - production infrastructure development.
- Production costs: Certain costs and expenses will be an inevitable consequence of the production of petroleum and its being made available at the wellhead (notably, day-to-day operating expenses and the costs of materials purchases), which could also include the costs of decommissioning (C4.3) where the producer pays amounts on account of future decommissioning costs under the terms of the upstream petroleum granting instrument, and also the costs of insurance (D6).
- Post-production costs: Certain costs and expenses could arise which relate to the produced petroleum, but only after the point of its production at the wellhead.[26] These 'post-production costs' could include the costs and expenses of:
  - petroleum gathering;
  - separating, treating and processing the petroleum to make it fit for sale;
  - compressing and transporting the petroleum from the wellhead to a further delivery point (including the possible provision of diluent); and
  - storing the petroleum.[27]

It does not necessarily follow that all of the costs and expenses which are associated with the production of petroleum will be deducted on an equal basis in the calculation of the royalty interest under an NPI. Deductible costs could be defined in the royalty agreement by a hierarchy of costs, where certain costs and expenses could be

"Production costs are the most obvious candidates to be taken into account as deductions in the calculation of payments which are due to be made to the royalty holder."

deducted ahead of the determination of the royalty holder's entitlement, and certain other costs and expenses would not be so deducted.

Production costs are the most obvious candidates to be taken into account as deductions in the calculation of payments which are due to be made to the royalty holder.

The royalty holder could require the NPI to provide that pre-production costs and expenses are for the account of the producer and will not be accounted for in the calculation of deductible costs from the payments which are due to be made to the royalty holder. The royalty holder could also argue that post-production costs relate to realising the commercial value of the petroleum, rather than to actually producing the petroleum, and so should not be deductible. Rather, says the royalty holder, these pre-production costs and post-production costs should be borne by the producer as an ordinary cost of doing business.

The producer could have a contrary view to the royalty holder, and could argue that pre-production and post-production costs are inevitably associated with respectively bringing the petroleum into existence and then making the petroleum fit for sale, and so should be deductible.

The definition of deductible costs in the NPI could provide as follows:

Deductible Costs means the costs or expenses which were incurred by the Producer in the relevant month of calculation and which were associated with:

(a) Production;

(b) the treatment, dehydration, and separation of the Produced Petroleum and the disposal of any associated waste water;

(c) the compression and the transportation of the Produced Petroleum from the wellhead to the Delivery Point; and

(d) the storage of the Produced Petroleum at the Delivery Point

provided that:

(A) any of the foregoing costs or expenses must be directly related to the Subject Interest and are allowable for deduction solely to the extent they were reasonably and necessarily incurred in connection with Production; and

(B) where a cost or expense is referable to more than one of paragraphs in this definition it will only be taken into account once for the purposes of determining the Deductible Costs.

Other production-related costs and expenses to consider in the definition of deductible costs could include the following.

Well workover costs: These are costs which take place after the production of petroleum has commenced, where the workover is intended to enhance production rates. These costs might have the character of pre-production costs, but they relate to the improvement of production after production has commenced (and could even be compelled by the royalty holder as a production covenant to be given by the producer (C8)). The royalty agreement could include the following as a deductible cost:

The costs or expenses which were incurred in connection with any well workover, well repair, well clean-up, well re-entry, well intervention, production logging, well stimulation or well re-drill (in each case to the extent carried out with the primary purpose of increasing the quantities of Produced Petroleum).

Overhead charges: Any overhead, administrative or indirect charges which are payable under the concessionary interests (or which are payable as a consequence of any law or regulation which applies in respect of the royalty agreement) which were incurred by the producer. The producer could require to deduct these costs on the basis that, without the incurrence of these charges and the maintenance of the concessionary interests, the production of petroleum would not have been possible.

Sales and marketing costs: Any sales, marketing, representation, agency, brokerage or hedging costs which were incurred by the producer in respect of realising the sales values of the produced petroleum.

Financing costs: The costs and expenses of financing the development of the infrastructure necessary to produce the produced petroleum (including interest payments, capital cost payments and arrangement and administration fees) which were incurred by the producer.

Financing costs are in the nature of pre-production costs and necessarily precede the actual production of petroleum, but their contribution to the production of petroleum in undeniable. The royalty agreement could provide for them to be amortised and for a defined amount to be worked into the royalty interest calculation for recovery by the producer. Once this door is open, however, it is possible that other pre-production costs could also be amortised and worked into the deductible costs equation by the same token.

Further issues to consider when defining the deductible costs under an NPI could include the following:

- Cost-recoverable costs: Whether the producer should be entitled to deduct costs and expenses where the upstream petroleum granting instrument takes the form of a production sharing contract (A4) and the costs and expenses have been, or will be, recovered by the producer in accordance with the cost recovery mechanism under the production sharing contract (in order to prevent a possible double recovery by the producer).
- Arm's length costs: Whether costs and expenses which have been incurred under a contract between the producer and an affiliated or an associated person (eg, a contract for the provision of goods or services which generate pre-production, production or post-production costs) should be rebased to an objective market value in order to prevent deliberate over-pricing by the producer and transfer pricing between the producer and the affiliated or associated person.
- Tax and royalty costs: Whether a producer should be entitled to make a deduction in respect of royalties and taxes which have been levied on the producer in relation to the produced

"One of the more common grounds for dispute between a producer and a royalty holder in relation to the terms of an NPI is whether certain costs and expenses which were incurred by the producer are or should be deductible costs under the royalty agreement."

petroleum (or its realised value) under the terms of the upstream petroleum granting instrument. These issues are addressed respectively at B5 and C12.2. The royalty holder would also want it to be made clear that the producer cannot deduct royalties which it has paid to other royalty holders under other royalty agreements.

One of the more common grounds for dispute between a producer and a royalty holder in relation to the terms of an NPI is whether certain costs and expenses which were incurred by the producer are or should be deductible costs under the royalty agreement. A royalty agreement could be very clear on what costs and expenses (whether they are related to the pre-production, production or post-production functions) should qualify as deductible costs. The problem comes where a royalty agreement uses lazy phrases (eg, 'the royalty holder will assume a proportionate share of the producer's costs and expenses which reasonably relate to commercialising petroleum') as an indication of what the deductible costs might be. This could generate a dispute between the parties over whether certain costs and expenses, albeit that they were incurred by the producer broadly in relation to the concessionary interests and the production of petroleum, should be deductible costs in the calculation of the amounts payable to the royalty holder. While the overall intention of such a general phrase might be discernible, the obvious lack of precision can be a fertile ground for disagreement.

In the quantification of deductible costs, the precise wording of the royalty agreement will be critical. Whatever petroleum industry custom and practice is in respect of the treatment of the various groupings of costs and expenses could be invoked to assist in resolving the dispute (C6.3), but the uncertainty which that inevitably entails will be a poor substitute for a properly drafted royalty agreement at the outset.

B5 Upstream petroleum granting instrument royalties

The producer could be obliged, under the terms of an upstream petroleum granting instrument (or under the terms of a prevailing mineral law under which the upstream petroleum granting instrument is granted), to pay an amount (which is sometimes also called a royalty) to the grantor. This royalty payment is typically determined by reference to the quantity of produced petroleum at the wellhead (net of any reductions to that produced quantity which are agreed to apply under the instrument). If the grantor elects to take this royalty in kind, the quantity of petroleum which thereafter remains at the wellhead will be available to the producer and its coventurers, to be taken as their respective entitlements.

Structurally, this would appear as follows:

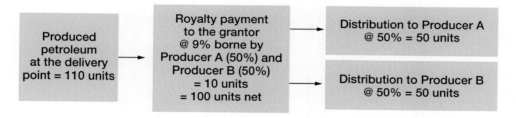

The form of the royalty interest which exists between the producer and the royalty holder will have a bearing on how the incidence of the royalty amount which is payable to the grantor of the upstream petroleum granting instrument is to be borne between the parties.

Under a GOR, the royalty holder could say that the obligation to pay the royalty to the grantor of the instrument is a matter entirely for the account of the producer, with the royalty holder having an expectation of the payment of a royalty amount which is based on the producer's share of the gross amount of produced petroleum, determined prior to and without any deduction to reflect that royalty.

Alternatively, in the calculation of deductible costs under an NPI, the producer could require that the principle by which certain taxation liabilities which are associated with the production of petroleum could be shared with the royalty holder (B4, C12.2) is applied equally to the producer's liability to pay the royalty to the grantor of the instrument.

Part C: Basic elements of a royalty agreement

This part considers the basic elements which are found in most royalty agreements, to support whichever economic arrangement from Part B is selected to apply between the parties.

Additional provisions which could be found in a royalty agreement, beyond these basic elements, are considered in Part D.

C1 Ambit

A royalty agreement could contain a number of statements which seek to characterise the intended nature of the relationship between the parties which the agreement creates, and what the royalty agreement is and is not intended to be:

1. *The Producer will provide the Royalty to the Royalty Holder (subject to the terms of this Agreement).*

2. *The rights, obligations and liabilities of the Parties under this Agreement are several and are not joint or collective. This Agreement is not intended, and will not be construed so as, to create a partnership or an association, nor to impose any joint or collective obligation or liability, and each Party will be responsible only for its individual obligations and liabilities as herein provided.*

3. *Except where otherwise expressly agreed, this Agreement is not intended, and will not be construed so as to provide, directly or indirectly, for any joint sale or joint marketing of the Produced Petroleum by or between the Parties.*

Royalty means the royalty interest which the Producer is liable for and which the Royalty Holder is entitled to under clause x.

Further definition of the ambit of the royalty agreement will be supplied:

- by a definition of:
  - the concessionary interests (A4);
  - the produced petroleum (A5);
  - the subject interest (A6); and
  - the royalty rate (A7); and
- by reference to:
  - the royalty agreement's duration (C4); and
  - any production covenants which the producer has given (C8).

An essential issue which must be considered early on is whether a royalty interest is intended to create a payment or performance obligation which is personal to the producer (which could be extinguished if the producer ceased to be a holder of the concessionary interests), or whether the royalty interest is intended to be an interest which will adhere to the concessionary interests (and which would ostensibly run to bind any successors or assignees of the producer in respect of the concessionary interests). This distinction is also reflected by the question of whether the royalty interest is a contractual arrangement between the parties, or whether the royalty interest creates a real property right.[28]

The royalty agreement could provide that:

The Royalty is a personal obligation of the Producer, which creates no express or implied real property interest in or charge or encumbrance over any of the Concessionary Interests in favour of the Royalty Holder or any other person. To the greatest extent possible under applicable law the Royalty [will] [will not] adhere to, encumber or run with the Concessionary Interests, and [will] [will not] bind or apply to the Producer's successors in title or assignees in respect of the Concessionary Interests.

or that:

To the greatest extent possible under applicable law the Royalty is and will be regarded as a real property interest which will adhere to, bind and encumber the Concessionary Interests, and which will run with, bind and apply to the Producer's successors in title and assignees in respect of the Concessionary Interests.[29]

In the latter case, the royalty agreement could contain wording which recites the need for a formal conveyance of the royalty interest to the royalty holder as a real property interest in order that the royalty interest is formally created and is made effective (C4.1).

The royalty agreement could also make provision that the royalty interest is to be registered and recorded on a cadastral register (D10) where the jurisdiction in which the concessionary interests are located allows such registration. Local registration could be necessary to perfect the real property title which the parties intend the royalty interest to create, and to this end the royalty agreement could contain a further assurances provision (C3) which could support this intention.

Whether the royalty interest creates a contractual or a real property interest is not a matter which can be freely elected between the parties.[30] Only certain jurisdictions[31] recognise the possibility of the creation of the royalty interest as a real property interest. Despite what the royalty agreement purports to say, whether the royalty interest is effective to create an interest in favour of the royalty holder which will adhere to the concessionary interests, and which in any event could run to bind any successors or assignees of the producer in respect of the concessionary interests, could be a matter which must be determined according to the law of the jurisdiction in which the concessionary interests are located. This could be addressed separately from the governing law which is selected to apply to the royalty agreement (C6.1).

C2 Audit and inspection

A helpful tool for the protection of the royalty holder's interests will be the right to audit the producer's operational records, to determine the accuracy of any production data or statements which are issued by the producer (C11) and to ensure that the royalty amount (whether it is payable in kind or in cash) has been properly calculated. This will be of especial importance where the royalty agreement takes the form of an NPI, as the royalty holder could wish to assess the veracity of the costs and expenses which have claimed by the producer as deductible costs (B4). To support this, the royalty agreement could oblige the producer to retain and make available all relevant books, records and accounts for a number of years after each year of petroleum production operations.

The royalty agreement could also set out certain timing conditions for the exercise of an audit by the royalty holder, and for the resolution between the parties of any discovered discrepancies:

1. The Royalty Holder will, at its own risk and expense, have the right on and from the commencement of Production to audit the Producer's (or any relevant Third Party's (including any operator's)) metering equipment, accounts and records relating to Production (including without limitation, all metering, measurement, forecasting, qualitative and sales data and sales contracts in respect of Production) and the Royalty.

2. The rights of the Royalty Holder under clause 1 may only be exercised during the year in respect of which the Producer's obligation to pay the Royalty arose and during the period of 18 months following the end of that year and will (except in the case of fraud) no longer apply thereafter.

3. The Royalty Holder will conduct an audit in such a manner as to minimise inconvenience to the Producer (and any relevant Third Party (including any operator)). The times of such audit and the number of persons participating therein will be agreed between the Royalty Holder and the Producer (each acting reasonably).

4. The Royalty Holder may not carry out, or have carried out, more than one audit in any period of 12 months and will keep all information and data disclosed to it strictly confidential and will not disclose the same to any person except to the extent agreed in writing with the Producer (and any relevant Third Party (including any operator)), nor will the Royalty Holder use any such information for its own commercial gain.

5. The Parties will use all reasonable endeavours to settle any issues arising from the exercise by the Royalty Holder of an audit within 90 days after the conclusion of such audit. A Party will have the right, on written notice given to the other Party, to refer to an expert appointed under clause [reference dispute resolution provision] any matters which cannot be resolved within such 90-day period.

6. The Producer will maintain or will procure that any relevant Third Party (including any operator) will maintain all accounts and records which are relevant to Production and the Royalty for a minimum period of 6 years from their creation.

Third Party means any person other than a Party.

It could be difficult for the producer to deny the basic need for this sort of provision in favour of the royalty holder, but the producer should be careful not to offer audit rights which the confidentiality and the data management rights of the concessionary interests could preclude the producer from being able to deliver. As a possible compromise, an audit function which is limited to confirming compliance by the producer with the essential commercial requirements of the royalty agreement could be performed by an independent auditor, rather than by the royalty holder itself, where there are sensitivities around giving the royalty holder an unfettered right to access to confidential information in respect of the concessionary interests.

The royalty holder might also require the right to make physical inspections of the sites at which the production of petroleum takes place. This could be related to verifying the accurate operation of the producer's petroleum measurement equipment (including witnessing periodic calibration exercises). The royalty holder might also feel the need to reserve a right to audit and to inspect the manner in which the producer carries out the petroleum production operations as part of the royalty holder's visible compliance with any environmental, social and governance commitments which it has made. Site visits which are made by the royalty holder will be at the royalty holder's sole risk and expense, and could be the subject of a mutual hold harmless liability allocation mechanism (C9).

"Site visits which are made by the royalty holder will be at the royalty holder's sole risk and expense, and could be the subject of a mutual hold harmless liability allocation mechanism."

C3 Boilerplate provisions

A royalty agreement will usually contain a number of customary administrative provisions, relating (for example) to:

- key definitions and principles of interpretation;
- a mechanism for the making of subsequent amendments to the royalty agreement;
- the giving and receiving of notices between the parties;
- the exclusion of third-party rights;[32]
- the incidence of costs and expenses which are associated with the negotiation of the royalty agreement (although the ongoing costs and expenses of administering the royalty agreement could also be argued to be deductible costs under an NPI (B4));
- the payment of interest (at a defined default interest rate) on unpaid amounts;
- the severance of invalid provisions from the royalty agreement; and
- a further assurances commitment of the parties to do whatever else may be necessary to effect the proper purpose of the royalty agreement.

The following administrative provisions could also appear in a royalty agreement, and could require some further thought.

C3.1 Confidentiality and announcements

The royalty agreement could state that each party will keep confidential the contents of the royalty agreement, subject to a list of customary permissible disclosures (including to auditors (C2) and potential transferees (C13), and which could include the possibility of registration of the royalty agreement (D10)), and that each party will not make any unauthorised announcements regarding the royalty agreement. This provision could be modified to state that even the fact of the existence of the royalty agreement will be kept confidential if this is important to either or both of the parties (although this could be at odds with any transparency or registration principles which might otherwise apply to the royalty agreement (D10)).

C3.2 Conflicts management

The royalty agreement could contain a conflicts management provision, which prescribes whether the royalty agreement or the concessionary interests (whether defined individually or as a whole) should have primacy if there is a common position between them which generates a conflict. This sounds simple enough, but such a provision requires careful consideration. An example of such a common position is how the consequences of a producer default which has implications under the JOA and under the royalty agreement (C10) is addressed.

C3.3 Entire agreement

The royalty agreement could state that it represents the exclusive agreement between the parties relating to the subject matter of their agreement and supersedes any other similar agreements or accords. Care must be taken with the application of this provision, however, where more than one royalty agreement in respect of the same concessionary interests is already in existence between the parties (or which could subsequently come into existence between the parties), which could always be a possibility. The royalty agreement might also provide that, where there is more than one royalty agreement in existence between the parties in respect of the same concessionary interests, those royalty interests will be treated as separate interests and will not be subject to any form of consolidation, cross-subsidisation or offset.

C4 Duration

Several issues will be relevant here:

- when and how the royalty agreement will commence and come into existence;
- the intended term of the royalty agreement; and
- termination of the royalty agreement.

C4.1 Commencement

A royalty agreement will ordinarily come into existence between the parties on the date when it is executed between them (A9), although application of the mechanics for the making of payment or for the delivery of petroleum by the producer in satisfaction of the royalty interest will inevitably be deferred where the concessionary interests have yet to move into the production phase. Those mechanics, and the royalty interest within the royalty agreement, will go live when the production of petroleum begins. 'Production' for this purpose could be defined in the royalty agreement as the commercial production of petroleum at a certain rate and for a certain period of time (after any commissioning and run-in activities have concluded), and could be configured to commence at the start of a month, to avoid the need for an apportionment where the royalty interest is calculated on a monthly basis (C11).

Matters which must be attended to in order to perfect the interest which is created by the royalty agreement (eg, the possibility of the formal conveyance of an interest to the royalty holder as a real property interest (C1) or registration of the royalty agreement (D10)) could be structured as obligations to be performed subsequent to the execution of the agreement, rather than as conditions precedent to the effectiveness of the agreement. On the other hand, the royalty agreement could be subject to a condition precedent in respect of the receipt of any necessary regulatory consents which might be required in respect of the agreement (unless such consents are secured by the parties prior to the execution of the agreement).

C4.2 Term

A royalty agreement, and the royalty interest which it creates, could be intended to exist for the lifetime of the concessionary interests to which the royalty agreement relates. In practical terms, this would mean the existence of the royalty agreement for the duration of the production of petroleum under the upstream petroleum granting instrument, subject to the following:

- **Extension:** The possibility of further extension of the duration of the royalty agreement if the duration of the upstream petroleum granting instrument is extended in accordance with its terms (and including the possible application of the royalty interest to any replacement of the original the upstream petroleum granting instrument (D11)).
- **Cessation of production:** The possibility of termination of the term of the royalty agreement where there is a permanent cessation of petroleum production and the introduction of decommissioning in respect of the last of the producing wells

"A royalty agreement, and the royalty interest which it creates, could be intended to exist for the lifetime of the concessionary interests to which the royalty agreement relates."

and associated infrastructure which service the royalty interest. From the royalty holder's perspective, this should be a genuine and permanent cessation of the production of petroleum from the concessionary interests, and not a partial or purported decommissioning exercise which in reality is intended to disapply the royalty holder's interests under the royalty agreement. The royalty holder will ordinarily have no control over the producer's decision to enter the decommissioning phase, unless this is a matter which is covered by a production covenant in the royalty agreement (C8).[33]

Where a rule against perpetuities could apply to, and could be violated by, the royalty agreement,[34] the royalty agreement could provide that the royalty interest will have the maximum permissible duration under applicable law.[35] This could be an issue where the royalty agreement is expressed also to apply to future or replacement upstream petroleum granting instruments (D11).

Alternatively, a royalty interest could be expressed to exist for a defined period of time, or until the royalty holder has achieved a defined return (whether measured in petroleum or in cash). This latter case is particularly so where a royalty interest is intended to repay an investment (A3.1):

1. *This Agreement is effective from the Signature Date and, subject to earlier termination by written agreement between the Parties or the expiry of the Concession, will continue in effect:*

   [until the permanent cessation of Production]

   [until the [•] anniversary of the Signature Date]

   [until payments made by the Producer under this Agreement equal or exceed US$[•]]

   [until the quantities of Produced Petroleum which have been delivered by the Producer under this Agreement equal or exceed [•]]

   whereupon (subject to clause 2) this Agreement will thereupon terminate.

2. *The termination of this Agreement for any reason will be without prejudice to any rights, obligations or liabilities accrued, incurred or outstanding prior to the date of such termination or expiry, and will be without prejudice to any terms of this Agreement which are expressed to survive termination.*

C4.3 Termination

It is always a possibility that the parties could agree to end the royalty agreement at any time and to unburden the concessionary interests, even if there is no provision for this in the royalty agreement. This could be done by the producer giving to the royalty holder a single monetary payment which buys out the remaining value of the royalty interest. The basis for doing this would have to be agreed by the parties at the time, unless the terms of a redemption right for the royalty holder (D9) in the royalty agreement are applied.

Whether a royalty agreement could be terminated automatically as a consequence of the producer ceasing to be party to the concessionary interests is considered elsewhere (C1), as is whether a royalty agreement could apply equally to any replacement upstream petroleum granting instrument (D11).

The royalty agreement could contain a termination right for the royalty holder which is based on the occurrence of a defined event of default (eg, an unremedied default (including a payment or a delivery failure) by the producer, or the producer's insolvency), but this could be illogical from the royalty holder's perspective, since the termination of the royalty agreement would do nothing to advance the ongoing economic expectation which it creates for the royalty holder (unless the royalty agreement also contains provision whereby the royalty holder's termination triggers a buyout payment to the royalty holder (D9)).

Correspondingly, a royalty agreement could contain a termination right for the producer which is based on the occurrence of a defined event of default by the royalty holder, which if exercised would give the producer an opportunity to rid itself of the royalty interest obligation. The royalty agreement might create relatively less in the way of obligation for the royalty holder (C7), but there could still be circumstances where an unremedied breach by the royalty holder could lead to a termination right for the producer.

A failure of the royalty holder to meet any of its continuing funding obligations under the wider arrangements which underpin the creation of the royalty interest (A3, E1, E2, E3) could also lead to termination of the royalty agreement.

The royalty agreement could also provide that either party has a right to terminate the agreement where:

- the other party has admitted or has been adjudged to have committed a breach of any applicable anti-bribery and corruption (ABC) legislation (which might also be a breach of a covenant (C8) or of a warranty (C14) under the royalty agreement);

- an event of *force majeure* (D5) has existed for a defined prolonged period;
- the production of petroleum (according to whatever test the royalty agreement applies – C4.1) has not commenced by a certain date; or
- a defined condition precedent (see above) has not been fulfilled by a certain date.

The royalty agreement could also provide that termination in certain of these circumstances could trigger a buyout payment to the royalty holder (D9) where the royalty holder is not the cause of the termination event.

If the royalty interest is intended to be an interest which will adhere to the concessionary interests, then the termination provisions in the royalty agreement might also recite the need to unwind the formal conveyance of the royalty interest to the royalty holder as a real property interest (C1) in order to ensure an effective termination. This might be regarded as an expectation under a further assurances provision (C3) in the royalty agreement, but would be better spelled out.

C5 Information provision

A royalty agreement could require the producer to give certain operational information to the royalty holder on an ongoing basis, relating, for example, to anticipated and ongoing petroleum production and the development and overall performance of the concessionary interests.

The royalty holder will say that it requires this information so it can have a more informed view of the performance of the concessionary interests and can better protect its expectations under the royalty interest:

1. *The Producer will give notice to the Royalty Holder as soon as practicable of:*

    1.1 *the submission to the Government of a field development plan to develop any part of the Concession Area, and the date requested by the Producer for the grant of consent to develop such part of the Concession Area;*

    1.2 *the expected annualised production profiles of Petroleum (of all types and grades) from the Concession Area; and*

1.3 the grant of any field development plan (or any other relevant consent or approval) by the Government relating to any part of the Concession Area.

2. *The Producer will give notice to the Royalty Holder not less than 90 days in advance of the anticipated date of commencement of Production from any part of the Concession Area.*

3. *The Producer will give notice to the Royalty Holder: (i) not less than 10 days in advance of the anticipated date of any temporary cessation of Production from any part of the Concession Area; and (ii) not less than 90 days in advance of the anticipated date of any permanent cessation of Production from any part of the Concession Area.*

4. *The Producer will provide copies of the following to the Royalty Holder:*

   4.1 by no later than the tenth day of each month, an estimate of the expected quantities Production from the Concession Area in the next occurring month and the expected prevailing market prices for Produced Petroleum during such month;

   4.2 as soon as reasonably practicable, any material notices issued by the Government in relation to any of the Concessionary Interests; and

   4.3 as soon as reasonably practicable, any information relating to any event or proceeding which could reasonably be expected to have a material adverse effect on any of the Concessionary Interests or to cause a reduction to or a cessation of Production.

Such information which is made available to the royalty holder by the producer would be regulated by the confidentiality provisions of the royalty agreement (C3.1).

In response to the royalty holder's request for such information, the producer could argue that it should not be required to give this information because the royalty holder is already adequately protected through what could be discerned by the exercise of the royalty holder's audit rights (C2), and also by the information contained in the monthly statement (C11). Furthermore, it is very likely that the terms of the upstream petroleum granting instrument and/or the JOA could prevent the disclosure of information by the producer of what is sensitive operational information to the full extent and in the manner which the royalty holder ideally requires. Consequently, the producer's undertakings in this provision in the royalty agreement could be heavily qualified by reference to the restrictions to which the producer is otherwise subject.

The royalty agreement could also reserve a right for the royalty holder to commission (at its own expense) the preparation of reserves estimation and/or facilities and engineering reports at any time in respect of the concessionary interests. The is something which the producer might be willing to countenance, but this would also need to be reconciled with the willingness of the producer's coventurers to assist in this process, and to allow access by a third party to what they could regard as commercially sensitive operational information.

C6 Governing law and dispute resolution

A royalty agreement should recite a governing law and should also recite a mechanism for the resolution of disputes between the parties relating to the terms of the agreement. Whether industry custom and practice could be applied to the resolution of a dispute between the parties should also be considered.

C6.1 Governing law

A royalty agreement will (or at least should) select and state the law which governs the agreement. The selected governing law will be applied to the interpretation of the royalty agreement generally, and in particular to the royalty interest, in the event of a dispute between the parties. Much in how the dispute will be resolved between the parties will depend on the applicable jurisprudence which is available under the selected governing law. Different laws could result in different outcomes in relation to the interpretation of disputed wording in royalty agreements and royalty interests.

The governing law which is selected could be the 'local' law of the jurisdiction in which the concessionary interests are located; or it could be what is sometimes called a 'neutral' law (ie, an abstract but comprehensive body of law which has no obvious connection to the concessionary interest, such as English law); or a combination of the two for certain purposes. Thus, a royalty agreement could primarily apply the local law, with the neutral law to apply if there is a lacuna in the local law. The scope for confusion and dispute is obvious.

The governing law could also be expressed to be a particular body of law which will principally apply to the construction of the royalty agreement, but with provision that an alternative governing law will have priority of application in respect of certain matters in the royalty agreement (eg, the actual creation of the royalty interest):

This Agreement will be governed by and construed in accordance with the laws of [insert jurisdiction]*, except that any determination relating to the creation, the nature, the registrability or the transfer of the Royalty will be made in accordance with the laws of* [insert jurisdiction] *as the location of the Concessionary Interests.*

Where a royalty interest is created in respect of the production of petroleum from concessionary interests which underlie more than one jurisdiction (eg, in respect of a royalty interest which relates to petroleum which is produced from unitised cross-border concessionary interests), it would be difficult to provide that the governing law would be the laws of both jurisdictions (at least, not without some attempt to manage the potential for conflict).

C6.2 Dispute resolution

A royalty agreement should recite a mechanism for the resolution of disputes between the parties regarding the agreement. The royalty agreement could provide that disputes are to be resolved by any of recourse to a competent court, recourse to arbitration or reference to a nominated independent expert in relation to specific aspects of the agreement.

The majority of disputes under royalty agreements (where the royalty agreement has been drafted with anything less than absolute clarity – which is often the case) tend to relate to two particular matters:

- whether and to what extent certain costs and expenses which were incurred by the producer will be counted as deductible costs in the determination of the royalty amount which is payable under an NPI (B4); and
- whether the royalty interest is a personal commitment of the producer or whether it will bind successors in title to the producer (C1).

The former dispute is perhaps better suited to resolution by an independent expert (which could be a petroleum accountant); whereas the latter dispute might better be suited to resolution through a more legalistic process which examines the true nature of the royalty agreement.

Additionally, disputes could arise where the royalty holder questions the veracity of statements issued by the producer (C11), which could be reinforced by the results of an earlier audit (C2), which might also best be left to an independent expert for resolution.

C6.3 Custom and practice

Although this will not be spelled out in the royalty agreement as an option, where there are deficiencies in the wording of a royalty agreement which result in a dispute between the parties, as an aid to interpretation, the parties could seek to introduce some commentary on prevailing industry custom and practice in relation to the elements of the royalty agreement which are in dispute to support their arguments.[36] An appeal to industry custom and practice is sometimes used, for example, to address a lacuna in the royalty agreement relating to the deductibility of certain costs and expenses (B4).

What 'custom and practice' actually means for this purpose will be debatable. Evidence of usage from a particular project, sector or contract form will not necessarily amount to custom and practice;[37] and identified custom and practice could differ between different jurisdictions (which could introduce conflicting opinions as to what the applicable custom and practice actually is). It is common in a dispute to cite custom and practice from any jurisdiction as being acceptable for application to the jurisdiction to which the royalty agreement relates. The application of widely sourced custom and practice will therefore be at odds with the specificity of the selected governing law of the royalty agreement.

C7 Performance, breach and liability

The producer is the party which is predominantly subject to obligation under a royalty agreement, since the royalty holder expects the delivery of petroleum or the payment of cash in accordance with the requirements of the agreement. Consequently, a liability for an unremedied breach of the royalty agreement is an issue which is addressed principally from the producer's perspective. Whether the producer could claim *force majeure* relief in respect of such a liability is considered at D5.

In respect of a cash royalty, a failure of the producer to make payment when due to the royalty holder will be self-evident and difficult for the producer to deny (at least where the producer has produced and sold petroleum and has not accounted to the royalty holder for the latter's share of the sales proceeds). This could result in a claim for a debt which is due from the producer to the royalty holder (to which default rate interest (C3) could also apply).

In respect of a royalty in kind, where the producer has produced petroleum but has not made the royalty holder's share available to the royalty holder, the royalty holder could make a claim against the producer for monetary damages for breach of contract in order to recover its losses. The extent of the damages which could be recovered by the royalty holder will depend on what the selected governing law of the royalty agreement (C6.1) says. This could lead to difficulties of quantification; and a particular issue will arise in respect of the exclusion (which could apply expressly in the royalty agreement or by the implication of the governing law) of what are broadly termed 'consequential losses'. The exclusion of such losses, if they are taken to mean the recovery of purely economic losses in the form of profit, could condition the royalty holder's ability to recover its expectations under the royalty agreement.

A more difficult situation in respect of a cash royalty arises where the producer has not produced and sold petroleum, or has produced but stored and not sold petroleum, so that there are no ostensible sales proceeds which are due to the royalty holder. This could make it difficult for the royalty holder to quantify the loss which it has suffered; and the same difficulty of quantification would apply in respect of a royalty in kind where the producer has not produced petroleum.[38]

To overcome these difficulties of quantification, the royalty agreement could make provision for the payment of liquidated damages by the producer in such situations. The payment of liquidated damages could obviate the difficulties associated with quantifying the royalty holder's losses, and also the difficulties associated with applying an exclusion to the recovery of consequential losses (see above), if the liquidated damages are recognised to effect an agreed pre-quantification of likely losses (based on a legitimate commercial purpose) which will bind the parties, without the further need to prove their reasonableness when compared with the quantum of the actual losses. This at least is the position under English law,[39] but different outcomes could ensue depending on what the governing law of the royalty agreement (C6.1) says.

A failure of the producer to produce petroleum when required by the terms of the royalty agreement could be more defensible by the producer than a failure to make payment when due, since such a failure could be caused by a reason which is beyond the producer's control. This could be so, for example, where a decision is made by the upstream producer consortium to suspend the production of petroleum which the producer is bound by (D12), or because of the existence of a physical condition which has impeded the production of petroleum. *Force majeure* relief could be sought by the producer in such a circumstance (D5), but more careful definition of the producer's obligation to produce petroleum (whether it is then to be sold or made available in kind) could be a better way of managing this risk. The royalty agreement could be drafted to provide that the producer's obligation to the royalty holder will be conditional upon the production of petroleum from the concessionary interests in the first place (A4) – so that the producer would not be in breach of the royalty agreement as a consequence of the non-production of petroleum in certain circumstances. However, this protection would also need to be read in light of any wider performance covenants which the producer has undertaken in the royalty agreement (C8).

In order to reduce the prospects for a producer default, the royalty agreement could also state that the producer will not be in default of its obligations where the producer is a defaulting party under the terms of the JOA and its coventurers have sequestrated its petroleum lifting entitlements in accordance with their rights to do so under the JOA. This is an example of a conflict between the ambition of the JOA and the royalty agreement which could need careful management (C3.2, C10). The same principle will also apply where the producer's rights have been suspended under the terms of the upstream petroleum granting instrument for a reason envisaged by the instrument.

Where there is an unremedied breach of the royalty agreement by the producer which gives the producer a liability to the royalty holder, as an alternative to making a claim against the producer, the royalty holder might be able to remedy the position if the royalty agreement envisages the provision of collateral support by the producer (D1); or the royalty holder could be entitled to exercise a conversion right (D2) or a redemption right (D9) in respect of the royalty interest.

A royalty agreement typically creates less by way of obligation upon the royalty holder, although the royalty holder could be subject to:

- an obligation to lift petroleum at the wellhead or at a further delivery point (A4);
- a confidentiality obligation (C3.1); and
- the obligation to make certain payments to the producer (C11).

Whether an unremedied breach of the royalty agreement by one party could give a termination right to the other party is considered at C4.3.

C8 Production covenants

The royalty holder will recognise that the continued production of petroleum from the concessionary interests which sustain the royalty interest is a critical issue. To protect its expectations, the royalty holder could require the producer to give a series of positive and negative covenants in relation to its management of the concessionary interests.

These covenants could appear as a long-form list in the royalty agreement:

1. *Subject to clause 2, the Royalty Holder acknowledges that the Producer is exclusively entitled to make all operational decisions*

relating to Production (but without prejudice to the Producer's obligations and the Royalty Holder's rights under this Agreement).

2. *The Producer covenants with the Royalty Holder that the Producer will at all times during the term of this Agreement:*

   2.1 *fully perform its obligations as provided for in this Agreement in relation to the Concessionary Interests;*

   2.2 *comply in all material respects with the requirements of the Concessionary Interests and maintain the same in good standing, full force and effect;*

   2.3 *take all steps to enforce its rights and pursue any and all claims and remedies under the Concessionary Interests;*

   2.4 *not do or omit to do any act or thing, or agree to or (to the extent that it is within its power to prevent) suffer any amendments or modifications to be made to any Concessionary Interest which would, or which might, hinder or adversely affect the Producer's ability to perform its obligations under this Agreement or the Royalty Holder's rights under this Agreement;*

   2.5 *not surrender, relinquish, forfeit or terminate the Concession at any time, nor accede to or accept any of the same, without the prior written consent of the Royalty Holder;*

   2.6 *comply with the Concession and cause the Concession Area to be maintained, used, and operated in compliance with all present and future laws, any permits, licenses and authorisations issued by the Government, any other orders, rules, and regulations of any regulatory, agency, and any policies of insurance at any time in force or required to be in force with respect to the Concession and Concession Area;*

   2.7 *comply with all applicable environmental, social and governance laws, regulations and conventions which apply in respect of the Producer and/or the Concessionary Interests; and*

   2.8 *not, without first obtaining the Royalty Holder's prior written consent, materially amend or modify any of the Concessionary Interests, terminate or accept the surrender of any of the Concessionary Interests or consent to, or otherwise accept, an assignment of any the Concessionary Interests.*

Alternatively, the producer could offer only a short-form and relatively generalised covenant to the royalty holder in the royalty agreement:

The Producer covenants with the Royalty Holder that during the term of this Agreement it will not do or omit to do any act or thing (including in respect of the Concessionary Interests) the object or the effect of which is or would be to deprive the Royalty Holder of all or any part of the Royalty.

If the concessionary interests are yet to begin producing petroleum, the royalty agreement could include a covenant that the producer will do all it can to ensure the commencement of production.[40] If the concessionary interests are already producing petroleum, the royalty agreement could include a covenant that the producer will at all times ensure the production of petroleum at the greatest possible levels, and will sell the petroleum for the greatest possible returns.[41] The producer could be reluctant to accept unqualified covenants of this nature, however, and could at least try to qualify such production covenants by reference to what a reasonable and prudent operator would do.

Covenants which promote petroleum production where the producer is the nominated operator of the concessionary interests could be more meaningful to the royalty holder than where the producer is not

"Covenants which promote petroleum production where the producer is the nominated operator of the concessionary interests could be more meaningful to the royalty holder than where the producer is not the operator."

the operator. In the latter case, the royalty agreement could additionally contain a covenant that the (non-operator) producer will seek to cause the operator of the concessionary interests to behave in a way which reflects the royalty holder's rights and expectations under the royalty agreement.

The undertaking of such covenants by the producer assumes that the producer is willing to be exposed to what could be regarded as operational interference by the royalty holder in the business of petroleum production. It also assumes that the producer actually has some say in how the production of petroleum is effected (which might particularly not be the case for a producer which is not the operator of the concessionary interests). In any event, the producer should not promise more in the covenants which it gives in the royalty agreement than it is actually able to deliver under the concessionary interests.

Some latitude for the producer in respect of the covenants which it gives could be offered in the royalty agreement:

> *In respect of the covenants which are given by the Producer in this clause x the Producer will only be required to take decisions and to act in respect of the Concessionary Interests where doing so would be in accordance with the standard of a Reasonable and Prudent Operator.*

The producer could also give various covenants which reiterate the warranties which it has given in the royalty agreement (C14), if the governing law of the royalty agreement (C6.1) is one which recognises warranties as promises which are capable of being given only in respect of current and historical facts and which are not capable of being given in respect of future behaviours. Specific covenants relating to compliance with applicable ABC legislation could be given by both parties (and, in particular by the royalty holder in respect of its application of the proceeds of sale of in-kind petroleum quantities and of cash royalty amounts). The producer could also give various covenants which reflect the agreed principles in the royalty agreement relating to the management of competing interests (D7).

Particular issues to note in respect of any production covenants which are given by the producer will be:

- the extent to which the royalty holder has a say in relation to the introduction of decommissioning of the concessionary interests (C4.3); and
- whether the producer should be obliged to undertake or to participate in exclusive operations under the JOA in order to maximise the amount of produced petroleum (A5).

The ability of the royalty holder to control the producer's activities under the concessionary interests through the application of the production covenants must also be viewed carefully in light of the legal and regulatory regime which is applicable to the concessionary interests and the royalty agreement. It could be that the element of control which is conferred on the royalty holder by these covenants could be argued to expose the royalty holder to certain liabilities in respect of the concessionary interests (A2).

A breach of a covenant by the producer could lead to a claim by the royalty holder for monetary damages for breach of contract (assuming that the royalty holder can prove and can quantify the loss which it has suffered because of that breach), or it could be considered as an event of termination of the royalty agreement (C4.3). Injunctive relief might also be ordered by a court to prevent an actual or a prospective breach of covenant by the producer.

C9 Production indemnities

The royalty holder will want to see the continued production of petroleum from the concessionary interests which sustain the royalty agreement. But the royalty holder is not party to those concessionary interests and, consistent with that absence of status, the royalty holder will not want to be exposed to any of the production-related liabilities which are associated with being a party. These liabilities could include exposure to:

- costs and expenses which are associated with the operation of the concessionary interests;
- third-party claims relating to the concessionary interests;
- general environmental liabilities;
- clean-up costs consequent upon a pollution event; and
- the eventual costs of decommissioning the associated petroleum production, processing, transportation and storage infrastructure (and also the costs of providing security in respect of those decommissioning costs).

The potential liability of the royalty holder for production-related taxation is considered separately in C12.

In the royalty agreement, the royalty holder could require a clear statement that the producer assumes (and that the royalty holder will have no exposure to) all production-related liabilities. The royalty holder could also require that this position be reinforced by an undertaking of the producer:

- not to pass through any such liabilities to the royalty holder; and
- to indemnify the royalty holder in respect of any exposure to

"If the producer does agree to indemnify the royalty holder, then the producer could require the right to take control of the defence activities in the event of a potentially indemnifiable claim being made against the royalty holder."

these liabilities to which the royalty holder could become subject (whether that liability of the royalty holder is to the producer directly or to a third party (which could also be a person which is related to the producer)):

The Producer assumes all liability in connection with the Production Liabilities. The Royalty Holder will have no liability (whether to the Producer or to any Third Party) in connection with the Production Liabilities. The Producer will fully indemnify and hold harmless the Royalty Holder against any liability which the Royalty Holder may incur (whether to the Producer or to any Third Party) in connection with the Production Liabilities (regardless of any negligence or fault on the Royalty Holder's part).

***Production Liabilities** means all claims, costs, damages, expenses, liabilities or obligations incurred or arising in connection with the Concessionary Interests and/or Production (including, without limitation, any and all liabilities for the costs of performance of the Concessionary Interests, claims made by Third Parties in connection with the performance of the Concessionary Interests, and liability for pollution remediation costs and decommissioning and decommissioning security costs in respect of the Concessionary Interests.*

__Third Party__ means any person other than a Party.

Care must be taken in the structuring of the indemnification of the royalty holder against all production-related liabilities to ensure that it does not inadvertently disapply the agreed exposure of the royalty holder to the costs and expenses which the producer is entitled to deduct from the sales proceeds under an NPI (B4).

In the above example, the royalty holder is the beneficiary of the producer's indemnity; but for more complete protection, the royalty holder could require that the producer's indemnity be given in respect of the loss or liability which might be suffered by any member of a much wider royalty holder-related indemnity group which includes not only the royalty holder, but also the royalty holder's affiliates, shareholders, coventurers, agents and contractors (and, in each case, each of their directors, officers and employees).

The producer's reaction to all of this could be to say that it is clear that the royalty holder is not directly a party to the concessionary interests, and that consequently the royalty holder will not be exposed to the associated liabilities and so should not need to be indemnified against those liabilities in the royalty agreement. As a counter, the royalty holder could point out that if the liability risk really is so remote, then the producer should be untroubled by giving the required indemnity.

If the producer does agree to indemnify the royalty holder, then the producer could require the right to take control of the defence activities in the event of a potentially indemnifiable claim being made against the royalty holder.

The royalty holder could insist that the presence of an indemnity from the producer in the royalty agreement could increase the necessity for the provision of collateral support in respect of the producer's payment obligations (D1).

The analysis in this section assumes that the royalty holder is not also a party to the concessionary interests, as a producer. If a petroleum project is structured so that the royalty holder is also a party to the concessionary interests (A3.2), then care will need to be taken in the drafting of the royalty agreement to ensure that the denial of liability and the creation of an indemnity in favour of the royalty holder is qualified to reflect that exact capacity, so that it does not affect the royalty holder's liability to the production-related liabilities for which it ought to be liable as a producer in its own right.

As a limited departure from the principle of the royalty holder being indemnified in all respects by the producer, the royalty agreement could contain an indemnity-backed mutual hold harmless liability allocation mechanism, to apply in respect of death or personal injury which is suffered by either party's personnel. This mechanism could apply, for example, in respect of site visits which are made by or on behalf of the royalty holder (C2).

C10 Relationship with the JOA

Certain aspects of a royalty agreement could overlap with the concessionary interests generally, and in particular with certain terms of the underlying JOA. In several places, care will be needed to ensure that the terms of the royalty agreement and the JOA are made consistent. An example of a common position which applies across both agreements is that of how a default by the producer under the JOA is addressed.

During the lifetime of a royalty agreement, the producer could become a defaulting party in accordance with the terms of the JOA. The customary immediate consequence of a continued default under the JOA will be that the producer's share of produced petroleum will be sequestered by the non-defaulting parties, meaning that there will be no petroleum available to the producer to meet the demands of the royalty agreement (whether the royalty agreement provides for a royalty in kind or a cash royalty) for as long as the default continues.

In the longer term, if the producer's default under the JOA continues, then the producer's interests under the upstream petroleum granting instrument and the JOA could be forfeited to the non-defaulting parties in order to remedy the default. In such a situation, the issue of whether the royalty agreement represents a personal payment or performance obligation of the producer, or whether the royalty agreement could be enforced successfully against the producer's successors in title that come to hold the concessionary interests (C1), would come to be tested.

There is likely to be little which the royalty holder could do to improve its position in respect of this interface between the royalty agreement and the JOA (although the provision of collateral support by the producer in support of its obligations under the royalty agreement (D1) could partially alleviate the situation for the royalty holder). It is particularly unlikely that the other parties to the concessionary interests would be willing to subordinate their rights under the default provisions of the JOA to give the royalty holder an improved right to recover its entitlements under the royalty agreement (whether ahead of or in equal measure to the application of their JOA remedies).

Other points of interface to note between the royalty agreement and the JOA will include:

- the definition of the producer's lifting entitlements to which the royalty interest will attach (A5);
- the ability of the royalty holder to audit and to inspect the producer's interests (C2);
- the overlap with pre-emption rights (C13); and
- the royalty holder's ability to secure operational information (D8).

C11 Statements and payment mechanics

In respect of a cash royalty, a royalty agreement will require the producer to submit to the royalty holder periodic statements which will relate to produced petroleum quantities (for royalties in kind and for cash royalties) and to realised petroleum values and associated costs and expenses (for cash royalties). Such statements are typically issued on a month in arrears basis:

1. *By no later than the fifth day after the end of each month the Producer will give to the Royalty Holder a statement (the Monthly Statement) which will contain the following information:*

    1.1 the quantities of Produced Petroleum for that month (showing also the relevant components of Crude Oil and Natural Gas);

    1.2 [for a GOR: the applicable Gross Values]

    [for an NPI: the applicable Gross Revenues for that month, and the Deductible Costs which are attributable to that month (showing also a breakdown of the relevant components by reference to the definition of Deductible Costs)]; and

    1.3 [for a cash royalty: the resultant Royalty (in US$)].

The royalty agreement could also provide that a statement could be presumed to be correct if its veracity is not challenged by the royalty holder within a defined period of time after it has been issued, but subject always to the royalty holder's audit rights (C2).

A royalty agreement should also set out a mechanism for payments to be made by the producer to the royalty holder (following on from the monthly statement, and assuming that payment is due monthly in arrears) under a cash royalty:

The Producer will pay the total amount shown in respect of any Monthly Statement which is due for payment to the Royalty Holder in full into the Royalty Holder's Account by no later than the tenth day after the end of each month.

The producer could, however, prefer to see a commitment in the royalty agreement whereby the producer is required to make payment of the royalty amount only when the producer has itself been paid for the petroleum which it has sold (B2)):

> *The Producer will pay the total amount shown in respect of any Monthly Statement which is due for payment to the Royalty Holder in full into the Royalty Holder's Account by no later than the tenth day after the day upon which the Producer has itself received the Produced Petroleum sales proceeds.*

The royalty holder could be reluctant to be exposed to the risk of non-payment by the producer's buyers in this manner (although, paradoxically, in other respects the royalty holder could be keen to have some say in the application of the buyer-producer relationship (B2)).

The royalty holder will require that all payments which are due to be made by the producer be paid in full and without setoff or deduction, to a nominated account. The producer, on the other hand, could require the right of setoff to apply to any amounts which are due for payment from the royalty holder to the producer, so that the producer would pay a net amount to the royalty holder. A setoff right would give the producer a limited form of collateral support in respect of any payments which are due to be made by the royalty holder under the royalty agreement.

Payments due from the royalty holder to the producer under the royalty agreement will be the exception rather than the rule; but such payments could be due, for example:

- where the producer performs certain transportation or processing activities for the royalty holder and expects reimbursement (B1);
- under an indemnity-backed mutual hold harmless liability allocation mechanism (C9);
- under a tax allocation indemnity (C12.3); or
- in respect of deductible costs where there is a negative royalty under an NPI which could give the royalty holder an actual payment obligation (D12).

Local taxation advice could be required in relation to whether the payment which is made by the producer to the royalty holder under a cash royalty would be a taxable supply on which some form of goods and services tax or value added tax would be due (and which could a require a suitable form of tax invoice to be delivered by the royalty holder, as the recipient of the taxable supply, to the producer).

C12 Taxation allocation

A royalty agreement should provide for an allocation between the producer and the royalty holder of the incidence of the taxation which could apply in respect of the production of petroleum and the payment of the royalty (whether in kind or in cash).

C12.1 The royalty holder's liability

A taxation liability could apply to the royalty holder in respect of the income which results from the sale of its petroleum share where it has received a royalty in kind, or to the income which results directly from the receipt of a cash royalty. An imputed sale by the royalty holder at a deemed value could be applied where the royalty holder directly uses its in-kind entitlements (eg, in a refining operation) rather than selling them.

C12.2 The producer's liability

A taxation liability could apply to the producer in respect of the revenue which results from the sale of the produced petroleum, from which revenue the producer would then pay the cash royalty to the royalty holder. Whether payment to the royalty holder which is due from the producer is calculated on a pre-tax or on a post-tax revenue amount will depend on whether the royalty interest is intended to be a GOR or an NPI (B2).

"A royalty agreement should provide for an allocation between the producer and the royalty holder of the incidence of the taxation which could apply in respect of the production of petroleum and the payment of the royalty."

Under a royalty in kind, the distribution of petroleum to the royalty holder could be treated as an imputed sale at a deemed value by the producer, so that the producer cannot evade the taxation liability which could otherwise be due in respect of the proceeds of sale under a true sale.

In each case, different tax treatment could follow if payment and receipt of the royalty amount (in kind or in cash) could be treated as the repayment of a loan which was made by the royalty holder (A3.1), rather than as income for the royalty holder or a sale by the producer).

C12.3 Taxation allocation

The simplest symmetry would be to say in the royalty agreement that the producer is responsible for all production-related taxation liability and the royalty holder is responsible for taxation related to receipt of the royalty amounts. Such an allocation of liability could also be backed up by a cross-indemnity between the parties:

1. *The Royalty Holder will pay, or will cause to be paid, all Taxes imposed upon the Royalty Holder in respect of the Royalty which is received from the Producer under this Agreement and will indemnify the Producer against any claims made against the Producer relating thereto (regardless of any negligence or fault on the Producer's part).*

2. *The Producer will pay, or will cause to be paid, all Taxes arising in respect of activities undertaken relating to the Concessionary Interests and/or Production under this Agreement and will indemnify the Royalty Holder against any claims made against the Royalty Holder relating thereto (regardless of any negligence or fault on the Royalty Holder's part).*

   *'**Taxes**' means all forms of taxation, duties, levies, imposts, charges and withholdings, direct or indirect, created or imposed by any taxation, fiscal or other appropriate authority and (without prejudice to the generality of the foregoing) includes: (i) income and corporate taxation, stamp on transaction tax or withholdings similar to or supplementing or replacing the foregoing or any of them; and (ii) all penalties, charges, interest, fines costs and expenses, and any loss of relief, allowance or credit, relating to any form of or claim for taxation or other imposition which is referred to in part (i) of this definition.*

The royalty holder could also require a grossing-up provision in respect of cash royalty amounts which it is due to receive where a taxation-related intervention (eg, the application of withholding tax) could reduce the amounts which are otherwise payable to the royalty holder:

1. *All payments due to be made under this Agreement by the Producer to the Royalty Holder will be made free and clear of and without any deduction or withholding for any Taxes; provided however that if the Producer is lawfully required to deduct or withhold any Taxes from such payments then:*

   1.1 the payments due from the Producer to the Royalty Holder will be increased as necessary so that after making all required deductions or withholdings the Royalty Holder receives payment of an amount equal to the amount it would have received had no such deductions or withholdings been made; and

   1.2 the Producer will make such deductions or withholdings, and will pay the full amount deducted or withheld in accordance with applicable laws and regulations.

The allocation of taxation liability under the royalty agreement which is suggested above is relatively simplistic. In practice, the suggested allocation will need to be reconciled with the specific incidence of taxation in relation to the concessionary interests in order to determine how quantities of petroleum which are made available (in kind or in cash) under the royalty agreement will be exposed to taxation, and where the incidence of taxation between the producer and the royalty holder should lie.

C13 Transfers

It is likely that during the lifetime of a royalty agreement, there will be the potential for the producer or the royalty holder to transfer its respective interests to another person. This is something which the royalty agreement should be careful to manage.

C13.1 Transfers by the producer

In respect of a transfer by the producer, there are two scenarios to note:

- a transfer of the royalty agreement and the obligations which it creates (to the extent that such a transfer, in the abstract from the underlying concessionary interests, is even possible); and
- a transfer of the concessionary interests which underpin the royalty agreement.

In either case, the royalty holder will be keen to preclude any transfer of interests by the producer which has the capacity to erode the value of the royalty interest to the royalty holder.

In respect of a transfer of the royalty agreement, the royalty holder could argue that the royalty agreement represents a personal payment obligation of the producer (C1), with the consequence that the royalty agreement cannot be transferred by the producer to another person. Even if such a transfer were to be possible, the royalty holder would be keen to ensure that the proposed transferee has at least equivalent financial status to the producer; and the royalty holder might also have commercial or political grounds for objecting to the proposed transferee. The royalty holder could therefore seek to include in the royalty agreement an absolute (or at least a heavily conditional) right of approval in respect of a potential transferee of the royalty agreement.

The rights of the royalty holder which could apply in respect of a transfer by the producer of the concessionary interests which underpin the royalty agreement will depend on the relationship between the royalty agreement and those concessionary interests (C1).

Where the royalty interest is a contractual right, rather than a real property interest, the royalty holder will require that if the producer transfers its concessionary interests, then the transferee will be bound equally to honour the terms of the royalty agreement as a direct replacement for the producer. It is not axiomatic, however, that the royalty agreement will adhere to the concessionary interests and so will automatically run to encumber the transferee. Consequently, such an arrangement would have to be expressly legislated for as a term of the royalty agreement[42] in order to reduce the risk that the transferee could disclaim the obligations which are associated with the royalty interest. Once again, the royalty holder will be keen to ensure the suitability of a potential transferee and so could require in the royalty agreement an approval right (whether absolute or conditional) in respect of a potential transferee. The producer could be reluctant to have its rights to transfer its concessionary interests constrained in such a way, however.

In either of the above scenarios, a particularly difficult situation could be created if the royalty holder wishes to object to a potential transferee which has otherwise been approved by the other parties to the concessionary interests.

In respect of a transfer by the producer (whether of the royalty agreement or of the concessionary interests), the royalty holder may also require:

- the right to compel an express undertaking of the transferee that it will accept and continue to honour the terms of the royalty agreement in favour of the royalty holder; and
- an acknowledgment by the producer that any collateral support which has been, or which is due to be, provided in respect of the

producer's payment obligations under the royalty agreement (D1) will not be diminished by the intended transfer:

1. *No transfer will be made by the Producer of an interest in or of any of the rights or obligations [under this Agreement] [in respect of the Concessionary Interests] to any Third Party without the prior written consent of the Royalty Holder.*

2. *Without prejudice to clause 1:*

   2.1 *no transfer will be made by the Producer of an interest in or of any of the rights or obligations [under this Agreement] [in respect of the Concessionary Interests] to any Third Party unless such Third Party has expressly undertaken to the Royalty Holder to be bound by the terms of this Agreement and unless such Third Party has demonstrated, if requested to do so, to the reasonable satisfaction of the Royalty Holder that it has the financial capacity for the performance by it of its prospective obligations under this Agreement, and has provided, if requested by the Royalty Holder, any additional financial security which the Royalty Holder might reasonably require in protection of the Royalty Holder's interests under this Agreement;*

   2.2 *no transfer made by the Producer of any interest in or of any of the rights or obligations [under this Agreement] [in respect of the Concessionary Interests] to any Third Party will operate to relieve the Producer of any obligation or liability with respect to such interest or rights or obligations so transferred which was incurred by, under or pursuant to the terms of this Agreement prior to the effective date of such transfer and remaining unfulfilled on that date. After the effective date of such transfer all obligations and liabilities incurred with respect to the interest or rights or obligations transferred, incurred on or after the effective date of the transfer, will become obligations and liabilities of the Third Party to whom such transfer has been made; and*

   2.3 *no transfer by the Producer of any interest in or of any of the rights or obligations [under this Agreement] [in respect of the Concessionary Interests] to any Third Party will operate to relieve the Third Party of the obligation to provide a [Parent Company Guarantee] [Bank Guarantee] as specified in clause [reference collateral support obligation], nor will it operate as a relief from any [Parent Company Guarantee] [Bank Guarantee] which was in place immediately prior to such transfer.*

   Third Party *means any person other than a Party.*

It could also be possible that a royalty agreement could provide for a pre-emptive right in favour of the royalty holder where the producer seeks to transfer the underlying concessionary interests:

> *If the Producer indicates a desire to transfer an interest in or any of the rights or obligations under the Concessionary Interests to any Third Party then, without prejudice to the requirement for the prior written consent of the Royalty Holder under clause [reference transfer provision]:*
>
> 1. *The Producer will give not less than 30 days' prior written notice to the Royalty Holder of the agreed commercial terms of a transfer by the Producer of an interest in or its rights or obligations under this Agreement to any Third Party, whereupon the Royalty Holder will have 30 days to elect whether to pre-empt such transfer (on the same commercial terms) and if the Royalty Holder so elects to pre-empt such transfer then the Producer will thereupon make such transfer to the Royalty Holder on the same commercial terms.*
>
> 2. *If the Royalty Holder does not make an election, or elects not to pre-empt, under clause 1 then the Producer will be free to effect the said transfer to the Third Party but only on the agreed commercial terms which the Producer notified under clause 1.*

From the royalty holder's perspective, this is similar in principle to the conversion right (D2), except that the royalty holder's right would apply to the entirety of the producer's interests rather than to a certain portion.

The ability of the royalty holder to apply a pre-emption right in respect of the concessionary interests will need to be reconciled with the potential application of any necessary consents and the waiver of any pre-emption rights under the JOA – which could operate to frustrate the royalty holder's ambitions. The royalty agreement might also make further provision for how such a pre-emption right would be applied in respect of the receipt of non-cash consideration by the producer as part of a transfer arrangement (including where the producer is engaging in an asset exchange), with recourse to an independent expert (C6.2) in the event of disputed valuations.

A proposed transfer of its interests by the producer could also trigger a conversion right (D2) or a redemption right (D9) in favour of the royalty holder.

C13.2 Transfers by the royalty holder

In respect of a transfer by the royalty holder, there are two scenarios to note:

- a transfer (of the whole or of a part) of the royalty holder's position as the royalty holder under the royalty agreement; and
- a transfer (of the whole or of a part) of the payment or production stream which is due to the royalty holder under the royalty agreement (but with the royalty holder remaining as the royalty holder under the royalty agreement).

A transfer of the royalty holder's position as the royalty holder under the royalty agreement could also trigger a redemption right in the producer's favour (D9).

In respect of a transfer of the payment or production stream under the royalty agreement, the royalty holder could wish to divert in its entirety, or to subdivide, the payment or production stream, so that the producer becomes obliged to pay or to deliver the payment or production stream to a third party or to a number of third parties. Where such a diversion of the payment or production stream is possible, the royalty holder will want the producer to make payment or delivery of the payment or production stream directly to the third parties, rather than that the primary payment or delivery of the payment or production stream is made to the royalty holder and the royalty holder then makes further payment to the third parties, because the initial payment or delivery to the royalty holder could expose the royalty holder to a liability to taxation on the full value of the payment or production stream (C12.1).

In respect of a partial transfer (through a subdivision of the royalty interest into a series of parts), the producer could be reluctant to accept the exposure to the greater level of administration which would inevitably result from the royalty agreement becoming held by more than one person as the royalty holder. The producer could also have a concern that any transfer of the royalty agreement or of the payment or production stream could be to a third party which is commercially or politically unacceptable to the producer. The producer could therefore seek to include in the royalty agreement an absolute (or at least a heavily conditional) right of approval in respect of any proposed transfer by the royalty holder.

C13.3 General

Either of the producer or the royalty holder could reserve the right to transfer its interests in the royalty agreement to a lender as security for financing purposes (which could create a permitted encumbrance (D7)).

If the royalty interest is intended to be an interest which will adhere to the concessionary interests (C1), then the transfer provisions in the royalty agreement could also recite the need for a formal conveyance of the royalty interest to an intended transferee as a real property interest, in order to ensure an effective transfer of interests.

C14 Warranties

A royalty agreement could recite certain warranties which are given by each of the producer and the royalty holder as of a particular date. These could be basic warranties:

- which relate to the capacity and the authority of each party to contract in the manner suggested by the royalty agreement;
- that the royalty agreement will not offend any other arrangements to which they are party (which, in the producer's case, will particularly be an issue in relation to the concessionary interests); and
- that no other consents or approvals (other than those which are already referenced in the royalty agreement (C4.1)) will be needed to allow the business of the royalty agreement to proceed.

Specific warranties relating to compliance with applicable ABC legislation could be given by both parties, and the producer could give warranties in relation to:

- its ownership of the concessionary interests;
- the management of competing interests (D7);
- the absence of litigation or disputes relating to the concessionary interests; and
- compliance with defined environmental standards.

The producer could also be required to warrant that the definition of the concessionary interests in the royalty agreement represents a true and complete statement of their form and status, and that there are no undeclared collateral arrangements.

The warranties provision in the royalty agreement would also be an appropriate location for the producer to disclaim the existence of any implied warranties which could be attributable to the producer. Such a disclaimer could relate to matters such as:

- the accuracy of any certification of the quantity of petroleum reserves in the concessionary interests or of any geological and geophysical data which the producer has made available to the royalty holder;
- the quality or composition of expected petroleum quantities; and

- anticipated petroleum production rates, recovery rates, petroleum prices, and associated costs and expenses.

Under English law, warranties are given in respect of present or historical facts, and are not capable of being given in respect of future behaviours (for which covenants (C8) would be required). The remedy for a breach of a warranty is a right of the party to which the warranty is given to claim monetary damages for the loss which it has suffered; but ordinarily, a breach of warranty does not give that party a right to rescind the agreement in which the warranty is given (which would have to be expressly provided for by the royalty agreement if required).

Part D: Additional provisions in a royalty agreement

This part considers certain additional provisions which could be found in a royalty agreement, beyond the basic elements of the royalty agreement which are referenced in Part C.

The ability of a party to secure any of these additional provisions in its favour will depend on the degree of leverage which that party has in the negotiation of the royalty agreement. Not all of the positions which are suggested in the following provisions will be readily achievable; nor are the following provisions always found in a royalty agreement.

D1 Collateral support

To assist the royalty holder in overcoming an unremedied payment or performance failure by the producer under the royalty agreement (C7), the royalty holder could require the producer's commitment that the producer will (at the producer's expense) procure some form of collateral support for the producer's obligations. This collateral support could take the form of a parent company guarantee (to remedy payment or performance failure), or a form of bank guarantee or standby letter of credit (to remedy payment failure), in each case with the royalty holder to be the nominated beneficiary:

1. *The Producer will provide to the Royalty Holder (on or before the Signature Date) a* [Parent Company Guarantee] [Bank Guarantee] *in favour of the Royalty Holder in respect of the Producer's obligations under this Agreement. The agreed form of the* [Parent Company Guarantee] [Bank Guarantee] *is attached at Appendix x to this Agreement.*

2. *In the event of the failure of the Producer* [to make payment to the Royalty Holder of any amount which is due for payment] [to deliver to the Royalty Holder any quantity of Petroleum which is due for delivery] *under this Agreement then (without prejudice to the Royalty Holder's rights at law or under this Agreement) and at the Royalty Holder's discretion the Royalty Holder may apply the* [Parent Company Guarantee] [Bank Guarantee] *to recover* [the unpaid amount] [the undelivered quantity].

Such collateral support could be provided from the outset of the royalty agreement; or the royalty agreement could provide for the later provision of collateral support by the producer if a particular trigger event (eg, relating to a defined deterioration in the creditworthiness of the producer) has occurred.

As an additional or alternative form of protection of the royalty holder's interests, the producer could be required to fund a bank account, which will hold a defined amount of money at all times and which can be drawn down by the royalty holder in the event of an unremedied payment or performance failure by the producer:

1. *The Producer will establish the Holding Account (in accordance with its terms) within 10 days of the Signature Date and will thereupon evidence the establishment of the Holding Account to the Royalty Holder.*

2. *The Producer will fund the Holding Account with an amount at a minimum equal to the Holding Account Value within 90 days of the Signature Date and will thereupon evidence the funding of the Holding Account to the Royalty Holder.*

3. *Once the Producer has complied with its obligation under clause 2 the Producer will not allow the amount of funding in the Holding Account to fall below the Holding Account Value at any time.*

4. *In the event of the failure of the Producer* [to make payment to the Royalty Holder of any amount which is due for payment] [to deliver to the Royalty Holder any quantity of Petroleum which is due for delivery] *under this Agreement then (without prejudice*

to the Royalty Holder's rights at law or under this Agreement) the Royalty Holder may make a withdrawal from the Holding Account of an equivalent value of the failed [payment] [delivery].

5. *If the Royalty Holder makes a withdrawal from the Holding Account under clause 4 the Producer will promptly restore an equivalent amount to the Holding Account.*

Holding Account *means an account opened with a reputable bank in the names of the Producer and the Royalty Holder which provides for: (i) the Royalty Holder only to be permitted to make withdrawals from the account in accordance with the terms of this Agreement; and (ii) the Royalty Holder to be permitted to enquire as to the content of the account at any time.*

Holding Account Value *means US$[•].*

A suggestion which is sometimes made in the negotiation of a royalty agreement is that the producer could give the royalty holder a form of step-in right (sometimes also backed up by the issue of a power of attorney by the producer to the royalty holder, to better enable the royalty holder to exercise the step-in right), whereby in the event of an unremedied payment or performance failure by the producer, the royalty holder would have a right to step in to assume the producer's position in the concessionary interests. This is not a practical suggestion, because of the necessity to secure the consents of the other parties to the concessionary interests in order to effect such a right, and for this reason this particular provision is rarely encountered in practice. A step-in right could also be particularly difficult to effect in favour of the royalty holder where the producer is also the appointed operator of the upstream petroleum granting instrument and of the JOA.

A royalty agreement might also seek to provide that the royalty holder could have some form of lien or other security interest over the producer's production entitlements under the concessionary interests, so that an unremedied payment or performance failure by the producer under the royalty agreement would entitle the royalty holder to sequestrate the producer's petroleum entitlements.[43] Such a right would have to be reconciled with the default management rights of the producer's coventurers under the JOA (C10), and those coventurers could be reluctant to subordinate their JOA rights to the royalty holder.

In contrast, the royalty holder has fewer payment and performance obligations under the royalty agreement (C7), and so the provision of collateral support in respect of the royalty holder is less common. The creation in the royalty agreement of a right of setoff to apply to amounts which are due for payment by the royalty holder to the producer (C11) gives the producer a limited form of support.

D2 Conversion rights

A royalty agreement could give the royalty holder an option to convert the economic interest which the royalty interest represents into a defined part share of the concessionary interests in certain circumstances.[44] The royalty holder would ostensibly exercise such a conversion right where the returns on offer from being a party to the concessionary interests would outweigh the returns to be made from continuing to be a royalty holder. The exercise of the conversion right could then result in the extinguishment of the royalty interest and the termination of the royalty agreement.

Such a conversion right could be exercisable votively by the royalty holder at any time. Alternatively, the conversion right could be exercisable only after a certain threshold quantity of royalty payments have been made to the royalty holder. The conversion right might also be exercisable as a reaction to an unremedied breach of the royalty agreement by the producer (C7), or as a reaction to a proposed transfer by the producer of its interests under the royalty agreement (C13.1).

Where the royalty interest was originally created as part of a sale of the concessionary interests (A3.2), care will need to be taken to ensure that, from an accounting perspective, the royalty holder's option to convert its royalty interest back into a concessionary interest at a later date does not undermine the notion of a true sale of the concessionary interests in the first place.

It is unlikely that the conversion of the royalty holder's interests under the royalty agreement would be for the entirety of the producer's interests under the concessionary interests, given the likely disparity in values between the royalty holder's and the producer's respective interests. The royalty agreement should therefore be clear to define the percentage part of the producer's interests under the concessionary interests which would be transferred to the royalty holder upon the exercise of the conversion right:[45]

1. *The Producer hereby grants to the Royalty Holder an option to acquire [•%] of the Producer's Participating Interest (the Conversion Option Interest) in accordance with the terms of this clause x (the Conversion Option).*

2. *The Conversion Option may be exercised by the Royalty Holder*

"A royalty agreement could give the royalty holder an option to convert the economic interest which the royalty interest represents into a defined part share of the concessionary interests in certain circumstances."

(or by an Affiliate of the Royalty Holder which is nominated in writing by the Royalty Holder to the Producer) and is subject to the following conditions:

2.1 the Royalty Holder (or its Affiliate nominee) may exercise the Conversion Option at any time after [the Signature Date] insert the threshold for exercise] by written notice to the Producer (the Conversion Option Exercise Notice); and

2.2 upon receipt of a Conversion Option Exercise Notice the Producer will assign and transfer the Conversion Option Interest to the Royalty Holder (or its Affiliate nominee) and will execute and deliver to the Royalty Holder (or its Affiliate nominee) such documents and take all such other actions as are necessary to procure the assignment and transfer of the Conversion Option Interest to the Royalty Holder (or its Affiliate nominee) at no cost to the Royalty Holder (or its Affiliate nominee).

3. *Upon completion of the exercise of the Conversion Option under this clause x this Agreement will (subject to [reference the termination survivorship provision]) thereupon terminate and will be of no further effect.*

Participating Interest means the Producer's share of the entirety of the rights, interests, obligations and liabilities which derive from the Concession as at the date when the Royalty Holder exercises the Conversion Option.

As it is drafted above, the conversion right applies to effect a conversion of the entirety of the royalty interest. A conversion right for the royalty holder could also be written to apply only to a part of the royalty interest (so that the royalty holder has the best of both worlds, by keeping a part of the royalty interest in place and also having a participation right in respect of the concessionary interests). Such an arrangement could be effected by the creation of a sliding scale of interests and conversion equivalents in the royalty agreement. Where a partial conversion right is effected, the producer's subject interest will be reduced and the royalty rate could be modified accordingly (A6).

The ability of the producer to grant an effective conversion right to the royalty holder in respect of the concessionary interests, in whatever form it takes under the royalty agreement, will always be subject to the application of any necessary consents and the waiver of any pre-emption rights under the concessionary interests, which could operate to frustrate the royalty holder's ambitions.

D3 Expropriation protection
A royalty agreement could make provision for protecting the royalty holder's expectations where an event of expropriation occurs in respect of the concessionary interests. This could include a requirement under the royalty agreement that:

- the producer keep the royalty holder fully advised of an actual or anticipated expropriation event; and
- the royalty holder be appropriately compensated from the proceeds of a resultant award of compensation which is made to the producer in respect of an expropriation event (where the 'Buyout Amount' which is referred to below is defined in D9):

1. *The Producer will promptly notify the Royalty Holder of any threatened or instituted proceedings for the expropriation, condemnation or taking by appropriation of all or any portion of the Concessionary Interests (an Expropriation). In the event of an Expropriation the Producer will, at the Producer's expense, diligently defend such proceedings, deliver to the Royalty Holder copies of all papers served in connection therewith, and consult and cooperate with the Royalty Holder in the handling of such proceedings. No settlement of such proceedings may be made*

by or on behalf of the Producer without the Royalty Holder's prior written consent. The Royalty Holder may (at its own expense) participate in such proceedings (but will not be obliged to do so).

2. *With respect to all awards, judgments, decrees, compensation or proceeds of sale in lieu of condemnation or Expropriation with respect to the Concessionary Interests which are recovered by or on behalf of the Producer (collectively, the Award), the Royalty Holder will be entitled to receive and the Producer will pay a portion of the Award* [which fairly reflects the Royalty Holder's expectations and entitlements under this Agreement] [which is equal to the Buyout Amount].

D4 Fiduciary duties

Fiduciary duties (which could be construed narrowly by reference to that particular term, or more broadly by reference to general duties of good faith and conscionability) will have different meanings in respect of a royalty agreement depending on what the selected governing law of the royalty agreement (C6.1) says. The governing law will have a bearing on the extent to which the royalty agreement could be subject to the implication of a fiduciary duty, and the extent to which the royalty agreement could be at all capable of modifying that implication.

"Fiduciary duties (which could be construed narrowly by reference to that particular term, or more broadly by reference to general duties of good faith and conscionability) will have different meanings in respect of a royalty agreement depending on what the selected governing law of the royalty agreement says."

Under English law, despite the apparent complexity which is applied in the definition of a fiduciary duty, and also in what constitutes a person as a fiduciary,[46] it is arguable that a producer is in the position of a fiduciary to a royalty holder because of the opportunity for the producer to make a profit for its own benefit (and at the royalty holder's expense) from the trust which is placed by the royalty holder in the producer's operation of the terms of the royalty agreement. This could include where:

- the producer acts as the royalty holder's agent for the sale of in-kind petroleum quantities (B1); and
- the producer sells produced petroleum to an affiliated or an associated person under a cash royalty (B2).

The consequence of this is that if the royalty holder can prove that it has been short-changed by the producer under the royalty agreement, then the producer could be liable to the royalty holder for a restitutionary remedy (eg, an account of profits, which addresses the gain which was made by the producer), rather than for a compensatory remedy (eg, damages for breach of contract, which addresses the loss which was suffered by the royalty holder).

The royalty agreement could have something to say about the extent to which a fiduciary duty could be said to be owed by the producer to the royalty holder by implication, which could then be modified by the royalty agreement:

> [To the greatest extent possible under applicable law] *This Agreement* [creates no fiduciary rights, duties or obligations and] *hereby excludes the creation or the implication of any fiduciary rights, duties or obligations which are or may be owed by the Producer to the Royalty Holder as a consequence of the Producer's obligations and/or the Royalty Holder's rights and entitlements under this Agreement.*

D5 *Force majeure*

A royalty agreement could contain a *force majeure* provision, by which an affected party could be relieved from the liability which it would otherwise have to the other party for an unremedied breach of the royalty agreement where the breach is caused by an event or circumstance which is beyond the affected party's reasonable control.

Force majeure relief could, for example, be claimed by a party where the continued performance of the royalty agreement would expose it to liability for a breach of sanctions which have been imposed which affect any of the concessionary interests, the royalty agreement or the parties. But in more general terms, the practical

"A royalty agreement could contain a force majeure provision, by which an affected party could be relieved from the liability which it would otherwise have to the other party for an unremedied breach of the royalty agreement where the breach is caused by an event or circumstance which is beyond the affected party's reasonable control."

necessity for a *force majeure* provision in a royalty agreement could be questionable.

A *force majeure* provision will ordinarily not excuse the failure of an affected party to make payment of money when due and so would offer no assistance to the producer which has failed to make payment under a cash royalty (unless the *force majeure* event which is complained of relates to the production of petroleum in the first place or has caused the producer's inability to actually sell the produced petroleum and to thereby realise any sales proceeds which could then be disbursed to the royalty holder – which might, for example, be a possibility in the case of the introduction of sanctions which disable the producer's petroleum sales ambitions).

In respect of a royalty in kind, a *force majeure* provision could operate to excuse the failure of the producer to produce and to deliver petroleum (which could also include the consequence of a production shut-in decision by the operator (D12)). However, the proper construction of how the producer's lifting entitlement is determined and how, from that, the measure of the produced petroleum (A5) and the producer's obligation (C7) is determined, could at the outset neutralise the risk of a failure to produce petroleum for which the producer could otherwise be liable.

The royalty holder has fewer obligations under a royalty agreement (C7) for which it could require relief under a *force majeure* provision, but such relief could be of relevance to the royalty holder's lifting obligation (A4). Payment failure by the royalty holder (in the limited circumstances where the royalty agreement could require the royalty holder to make payment (C11)) would not ordinarily qualify for *force majeure* relief.

D6 Insurance

The producer will ordinarily be the beneficiary of insurance protection in respect of the assets which underpin the concessionary interests (and the maintenance of such insurance could also be a production covenant to which the producer is subject (C8)).

The royalty holder could argue that:

- it should be named as a coinsured person on the policy of insurance, in recognition of the economic interest which the royalty holder has; and/or
- the producer must undertake to apply the proceeds of insurance to a reinstatement of any physical infrastructure and assets which are lost or damaged (rather than that the producer can apply those proceeds for any other purpose), in the interests of preserving the value of the royalty interest.

D7 Management of competing interests

In order to give primacy to the royalty holder's expectations in respect of the royalty interest, the royalty holder could require the producer to warrant in the royalty agreement (C14) that no other royalty agreements (or any similar arrangements) exist in respect of the producer's interests in the concessionary interests at the time of entry into the royalty agreement:

> *The Producer warrants to the Royalty Holder that* [as of the Signature Date] [in respect of each day during the Term]*, except for this Agreement and any royalty lawfully imposed by the Government under the Concessionary Interests, there is no royalty interest, carried interest, production payment, net profit interest, net revenue interest, claim, overriding interest, lien, encumbrance or other similar burden existing or created over the Producer's interests in the Concessionary Interests, nor is there in effect any agreement or commitment to create any of the foregoing.*

The royalty holder could also require the producer to covenant (C8) not to create any other royalty agreements (or other arrangements such as liens or charges) in respect of the producer's interests in the concessionary interests after the date of entry into the royalty agreement:

The Producer covenants to the Royalty Holder that, except for this Agreement, it will not create or permit to be created any other royalty interest, carried interest, production payment interest, net profit interest, net revenue interest, claim, overriding interest, lien, encumbrance or other similar burden over the Concessionary Interests during the Term [except with the prior written consent of the Royalty Holder [such consent not to be unreasonably withheld or delayed]] [except where such other interest or burden as aforesaid is expressly subordinated to the Royalty Holder's interests under this Agreement].

The producer's covenant to the royalty holder (if such a covenant is even offered) could be absolute or it could be subject to certain conditions, including the possible subordination of any later arrangements to the royalty interest.

The producer would have to satisfy itself that as a matter of fact, it is able to give the warranty which is suggested above, and could be reluctant to give the covenant which is suggested above because of the obvious constraints which it would impose on the ongoing conduct of the producer's business. A particular issue to note is the relationship between the royalty holder's interests and the default management rights of the producer's coventurers under the JOA (C10), where the producer's coventurers could be reluctant to subordinate their JOA rights to the royalty holder.

Despite the royalty holder's expectations as to the primacy of the royalty interest, the royalty agreement could also set out a series of permitted encumbrances to which the royalty holder's interests would be subject. This list could include:

- any identified pre-existing encumbrances;
- encumbrances which apply in favour of the grantor under the terms of the upstream petroleum granting instrument; and
- other statutory encumbrances (including those which cannot be derogated from by the producer).

Where the producer is party to a number of different concessionary interests in a particular jurisdiction and the royalty interest relates to only one of those concessionary interests, the royalty holder could require that any curtailments of petroleum production which affect those concessionary interests as a whole be borne rateably across all of the concessionary interests, and that the concessionary interests to which the royalty interest relates not be disproportionately burdened.

D8 Pooling and unitisation
During the lifetime of a royalty agreement, the concessionary interests

could become the subject of a pooling or a unitisation exercise, and the royalty interest would be determined by reference to the concessionary interests (A4) and the producer's subject interests (A6) which result from the outcome of the pooling or the unitisation exercise.

The royalty holder could be concerned that such an exercise could have an adverse effect on the royalty holder's interests under the royalty agreement. Consequently, the royalty agreement could contain a relatively lengthy provision which affords certain rights to the royalty holder in respect of the undertaking of such an exercise:

1. *The Producer reserves the right at any time and from time to time to enter into arrangements for the pooling of Production with production from other concession areas or the unitisation of any part of the Concession Area with another block or blocks covering areas adjacent to the Concession Area, in order to comply with the requirements of the Government or when in the judgement of the Producer such pooling or unitisation would be consistent with the practice of a Reasonable and Prudent Operator.*

2. *The Royalty will be calculated pursuant to the terms of this Agreement according to that portion of Production which is allocated to the Concession Area under the terms of any agreement referred to in clause 1.*

3. *The Producer undertakes to act in the best interests of the Royalty Holder in effecting any such pooling or unitisation and will as soon as reasonably practicable notify to the Royalty Holder the interest which is to be held by the Producer in the Concession Area pursuant to any agreed pooling arrangement or unitisation arrangement and, thereafter, any revisions to such interest pursuant to any re-determination or modification.*

4. *If the Royalty Holder does not believe that the interest which is to be held by the Producer in the Concession Area pursuant to any agreed pooling arrangement or unitisation arrangement protects the best interests of the Royalty Holder or is otherwise fair and equitable then the Royalty Holder will (at its own expense) have the right to obtain the determination of a suitably qualified independent expert on what the correct interest should have been. The Producer will grant the expert free access to all seismic and well data which may be needed for the expert to make its determination.*

5. *If the expert (in the absence of fraud or manifest error)*

determines that an interest which is greater than that proposed by the Producer should apply then that interest will apply for the purpose of calculation of the Royalty.

Alternatively, a shorter-form provision to address this situation might be recited in the royalty agreement:

The Royalty will not in any way be reduced or adversely affected by any pooling or unitisation agreement which is entered into by the Producer in respect of or otherwise relating to any part of the Concession Area.

On the other hand, the royalty agreement could say nothing which inhibits the producer's ability to undertake a pooling or a unitisation exercise as it sees fit. It is not realistic to expect that the royalty holder will have the ability to stop, or to exercise significant control over the performance of, a pooling or a unitisation exercise; but the producer could be obliged to have some measure of regard for the interests of the royalty holder.

A particular issue for the royalty holder will be to secure an acknowledgment from the producer that the definition of the unitised areas is not subject to a side agreement whereby the producer has accepted a pool or a unit interest which was less than the geological and geophysical data merited in exchange for another inducement. This could be made the subject of a covenant (C8) or of a warranty (C14) within the royalty agreement

D9 Redemption rights
A royalty agreement could provide that if the royalty holder seeks to transfer the entirety of its interests in the royalty agreement to another person (C13.2), the producer will have a right to redeem the royalty interest by buying out the royalty holder's position (so extinguishing the royalty agreement) according to a defined valuation formula. This redemption right might be of particular value to the producer where the producer has an aversion to the royalty holder's proposed transferee.

The royalty holder's concern that it might lose out on the future value of the royalty interest through the exercise of such a redemption right by the producer will abate if the valuation formula is calculated to be sufficient to protect the royalty holder's loss of expectation:

Where the Royalty Holder gives notice to the Producer of its intention to transfer all (but not part) of its interests under this Agreement to any person under clause [reference the royalty holder's transfer right provision] *the Producer may within 30 days*

of receipt of the Royalty Holder's notice give notice to the Royalty Holder (which latter notice will be irrevocable by the Producer once given) of its intention to exercise the Buyout Option, and whereupon: (i) the Producer will pay the Buyout Amount to the Royalty Holder within 30 days of the date of the Producer's notice; and (ii) this Agreement will (subject to [reference the termination survivorship provision]) thereupon terminate and will be of no further effect.

Buyout Option *means the option of the Producer buy out the Royalty Holder's interests in accordance with this clause x.*

Buyout Amount *means payment by the Producer to the Royalty Holder of an amount (expressed in US$) calculated as:*

$$A = B \times C \times \bullet \% \ ^{47}$$

where:

A means the amount of the payment which is due from the Producer to the Royalty Holder under this formulation;

B means the arithmetic average of the amounts paid by the Producer to the Royalty Holder under this Agreement in respect of the last complete calendar year preceding the year in which the Buyout Amount calculation is determined;[48] and

C means the lesser of: (i) the number of calendar years remaining on the Concession after the year in which the Buyout Amount calculation is determined; and (ii) • years.

The royalty agreement could also provide that if the producer seeks to transfer its interests in the concessionary interests to another person (C13.1), or if the producer commits an unremedied breach of the royalty agreement (C7), the royalty holder will have a right to have the royalty interest redeemed by the producer (and so to extinguish the royalty agreement) according to the same valuation formula.

Where a royalty interest is structured so as to give a defined long-term monetary return to an investor as the royalty holder (A3.1), the royalty agreement could contain a right of the royalty holder to accelerate the recovery of its interests by obliging the producer to buy out the remainder of the royalty interest at any time by making a lump-sum payment to the royalty holder. This payment could be of a sum which is calculated to reflect the unredeemed monetary value of the royalty interest following the buy out amount mechanism suggested above, and so including a discount factor which is intended to reflect the benefit of the accelerated recovery which is being made by the royalty holder. Such a mechanism for making an accelerated recovery could be helpful to the royalty holder where there are concerns about the long-term prospectivity of the concessionary interests and the ability of those interests to fully satisfy the royalty holder's expectations of making a full recovery of its investment through the royalty interest.

Whether the producer should have the same open right to redeem the royalty interest will be a matter for negotiation.

D10 Registration

The royalty holder will be keen to ensure that the royalty agreement binds the producer and the concessionary interests to which it relates to the greatest extent possible. This is principally so that any successors in title to or assignees of the producer (C13.1) will have notice of the existence of the royalty agreement and will be equally bound by it in favour of the royalty holder (to the extent that the royalty agreement represents anything other than a purely personal payment or performance obligation of the producer, and is intended to apply to the producer's successors or assignees (C1)).

The ambition of the royalty holder in this regard would be assisted by an open notification of the existence of the royalty agreement, which

"The royalty holder will be keen to ensure that the royalty agreement binds the producer and the concessionary interests to which it relates to the greatest extent possible."

could be effected through the public registration of the royalty agreement (wherever this is possible). Either of the royalty holder or the producer could also wish to effect a public registration of the royalty agreement in order to comply with any extractive industries transparency commitments to which it may be subject.

The public registration of the royalty agreement for either of the preceding reasons may be easier said than done, and the options for such registration might not always be adequate from the royalty holder's or the producer's perspective. Cadastral systems which would permit the registration of a royalty agreement are relatively rare; and even where they do exist, they tend to be localised and applicable to real property interests.[49]

The extent to which a royalty agreement can be recorded and publicly viewed (whether as an encumbrance on the concessionary interests or as an encumbrance against the producer, or generally for transparency purposes) will vary between different jurisdictions. It could be that the royalty agreement remains an essentially private arrangement between the producer and the royalty holder which is incapable of public registration in the manner which is suggested below:

1. *The Producer acknowledges that the Royalty Holder may at any time register or deregister the Royalty and/or this Agreement in any appropriate registry and hereby consents to (and will provide all reasonable assistance to facilitate) any such registration or deregistration.*

2. *The Royalty Holder acknowledges that the Producer may at any time register or deregister the Royalty and/or this Agreement in any appropriate registry and hereby consents to (and will provide all reasonable assistance to facilitate) any such registration or deregistration.*

3. *The registration, deregistration or non-registration of the Royalty and/or this Agreement by either Party at any time will be without prejudice to the rights, obligations or interests of the Parties under this Agreement.*

D11 Replacement upstream petroleum granting instruments

A royalty interest applies in respect of the defined concessionary interests, with the upstream petroleum granting instrument at the heart of those interests (A4). As a continuation of the royalty holder's expectations, the royalty interest could be expressed to apply to a replacement upstream petroleum granting instrument which is granted to the producer (in respect of the same area of the original upstream petroleum granting instrument or in respect of any part of that area), where the original upstream petroleum granting instrument has been surrendered by the producer or has otherwise come to an end:[50]

1. *The Producer will give notice to the Royalty Holder as soon as practicable of any forfeiture, surrender or termination of, or of any circumstances which may give rise to the forfeiture, surrender or termination of, all or any part of the Concession.*

2. *The terms of this Agreement will apply equally to any Replacement Concession and (but without prejudice to the validity of the foregoing) the Royalty Holder may require the Producer to execute a deed of assumption confirming that the terms of this Agreement will apply equally to any Replacement Concession.*

   Replacement Concession *means any new concession which is issued to the Producer (or to any of its Affiliates) in respect of all or any part of the Concession Area [within [•] years][51] following the termination, surrender or forfeiture of the Concession.*

It will not necessarily follow that the percentage size of the subject interest (A6) which the producer has in respect of the replacement upstream petroleum granting instrument will be the same as that which the producer had under the original upstream petroleum granting instrument. To ensure a consistent relativity of interests, the royalty rate (A7) could be resized (either upwards or downwards) to reflect the change to the size of the producer's subject interest under the replacement upstream petroleum granting instrument.

D12 Suspension rights

The producer could find itself compelled to produce petroleum (whether for delivery directly in kind or for sale for the payment of cash to the royalty holder) in circumstances where the continued production of petroleum is not economically sustainable for the producer. This could occur because the costs and expenses which are associated with petroleum production outweigh the revenues which accrue from the sale of petroleum; or because those revenues, while they are positive compared to the associated costs and expenses, do not generate a level of return which the producer would regard as being sufficient to merit continued operation.

The producer could also be exposed to the risk of a production shut-in decision being made on economic grounds (particularly where the producer is not the operator of the concessionary interests or otherwise might be unable to control or influence the making of such a decision) which might not relieve the producer of its obligation to deliver or to pay royalty amounts to the royalty holder (C7). The extent to which the producer could be exposed in these circumstances will depend on how the royalty agreement is written – including whether there is the possibility of *force majeure* relief (D5) for the producer.

Furthermore, to worsen the position from the producer's perspective, the royalty agreement could compel the producer to do the best it can in terms of petroleum production by including a commitment that the producer will, at all times, ensure that the production of petroleum is effected at the greatest possible levels as an additional production covenant (C8).

The royalty agreement could be written to recognise these risks to the producer, by provision, for example, for a suspension of the producer's obligations in certain circumstances (in this example, in respect of a cash royalty):

> *The Producer's obligation to pay the Royalty in accordance with the terms of this Agreement will not apply where and for so long as the Deductible Costs are equal to or are greater than [•] % of the Gross Values for such Crude Oil or Natural Gas.*

The royalty agreement could also recognise that the producer is subject to the risk of being compelled to implement a production shut-in decision. If the producer is the operator of the concessionary interests, then the producer's commitment to ensure the production of petroleum at the greatest possible level could be made subject to the right of the producer to behave in accordance with the standard of a reasonable and prudent operator, which standard would be defined in the royalty agreement; or the commitment could be made subject to operational decisions which are made under the concessionary interests and by which the producer is bound.

It could be possible that, in respect of an NPI (B4), depending on how it is worded, the realised sale price for the produced petroleum is less than the quantum of the deductible costs (because of low petroleum prices and/or high levels of deductible costs), so that the royalty holder could be due to receive a negative amount. The royalty holder could even be notionally liable to reimburse a share of the deductible costs to the producer. This is sometimes described as a 'negative royalty'. An actual payment from the royalty holder to the producer is unlikely in this scenario. Rather, the notional amount of the royalty holder's liability could be carried forward and offset against future royalty payments to which the royalty holder is entitled.

To avoid this risk, the royalty holder could require provision in the royalty agreement that if such a situation arises, the producer's obligation to pay the royalty amounts (and the royalty holder's corresponding obligation to assume effective responsibility for the associated costs and expenses) is suspended.

As an alternative to creating such a right of suspension, an NPI could be structured so that a running account (in the name of the royalty holder, so that it is insulated from the risk of the producer's insolvency) is established in the royalty holder's favour, into which will be credited positive gross amounts which are due to accrue in the royalty holder's favour, and from which will be debited the royalty holder's share of the costs and expenses for which it has agreed to be liable. There would then be a periodic cash sweep of the account in the royalty holder's favour where the net amount in the account is a positive figure.

Part E: Related arrangements

This part considers certain petroleum project interest transfer, financing and development arrangements which could entail the use of, or which in certain circumstances could recite certain of the terms of, a royalty interest.

Some of these arrangements will exist within the auspices of a farmout agreement, under which the producer is the farmor and the farmor's counterpart (to which an interest in the concessionary interests is transferred by the farmor under the terms of the farmout agreement) is the farmee.

The arrangements which are considered below are not mutually exclusive. An explanation of these arrangements is offered here to illustrate how they could function; in reality, a particular arrangement for the transfer, financing or development of a petroleum project could recite some combination of or reconfiguration of these arrangements, according to whatever best meets the commercial needs of the parties.

E1 Royalty-repaid carry costs
In a royalty-repaid carry costs arrangement, the following sequence of events will take place under a farmout agreement (typically in relation to concessionary interests which are still in the exploration and appraisal phase, before the production of petroleum has commenced):

- The farmor transfers a defined part of its concessionary interests to the farmee, in exchange for an upfront payment by the farmee;[52]
- The farmee meets the costs and expenses of carrying out the petroleum exploration, development and operational activities which are due for payment going forward in relation to the share of the concessionary interests which were transferred to the farmee, and also meets the costs and expenses which would otherwise be due to be met by the farmor in respect of its retained share of the concessionary interests – where the farmee is said to be 'carrying' the farmor's costs and expenses, and the amounts which are so met on the farmor's behalf by the farmee will be the 'carried costs'; and
- When the production of petroleum from the concessionary interests begins, the farmor will (from the realised value of the farmor's share of the produced petroleum under the concessionary interests) repay the carried costs to the farmee through the payment of a defined royalty. The royalty interest in favour of the farmee will come to an end only when the farmee has recovered the full value of the carried costs.

Structurally, this would appear as follows:

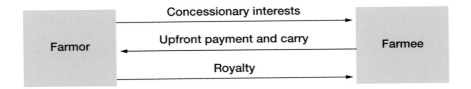

The farmee will want the royalty interest to keep paying out for as long as possible, and to this end the farmee could seek to apply an expansive definition of the carried costs which are due for repayment by the farmor as royalty amounts. The carried costs should be capable of clear quantification under the farmout agreement; but this is not always the case, and dispute could follow between the parties as to what costs and expenses the farmee should be able to recover under the royalty interest. This dispute would be similar to the determination of deductible costs in relation to an NPI (B4).

E2 Payout arrangements
In a payout arrangement, the following sequence of events will take place under a farmout agreement (again, typically in relation to concessionary interests which are still in the exploration and appraisal phase, before the production of petroleum has commenced):

- The farmor transfers a defined part of its concessionary

interests to the farmee, in exchange for an upfront payment by the farmee;[53]

- Each of the farmor and the farmee undertake to meet their respective shares (determined in proportion to the extent of the concessionary interests which they each hold) of the costs and expenses of carrying out the petroleum exploration, development and operational activities under the concessionary interests which are due for payment going forward; and

- When the production of petroleum from the concessionary interests begins, the farmee will (as additional consideration payable to the farmor, with payment made from the realised value of the farmee's share of the produced petroleum under the concessionary interests) pay a defined royalty amount to the farmor.

Structurally, this would appear as follows:

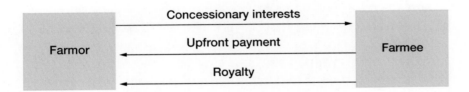

At the point in time when the farmee has (from the revenues which accrue from the production of petroleum, net of the royalty amounts which were payable to the farmor) recovered the costs and expenses which it incurred in connection with the petroleum exploration, development and operational activities under the concessionary interests which it farmed into – a one-time event which is often called the 'payout point'[54] – then (in recognition that the risk to the farmee of not recouping those costs and expenses has passed) the balance of risk and reward between the farmor and the farmee will be altered by provision that a royalty uplift after payout, or a back-in after payout, will thereafter apply:

Royalty uplift after payout – the royalty rate for the royalty which is payable by the farmee is set at a lower percentage for the period up to the payout point. Once that payout point has been reached the percentage of the royalty rate will increase for the remainder of the term of the royalty interest.[55]

Back-in after payout – the farmor will have an option to convert its royalty interest back into a defined share of the concessionary interests after the payout point has arisen (the 'back-in'), thereby extinguishing the royalty interest.

In each of the royalty uplift after payout and back-in after payout arrangements, the farmee has an obvious commercial incentive to defer the payout point for as long as possible, so that the farmee can continue to pay the lower royalty rate to the farmor (or not pay the royalty amount at all where a royalty holiday applies); or so that the farmee can keep hold of a larger share of the concessionary interests for longer. The farmor has the opposite incentives, with a desire for royalty amounts payable at the higher royalty rate or the ability to secure a reversion of a share of the concessionary interests arising at the earliest opportunity.

Where the payout point is defined clearly in the farmout agreement,[56] the relevant post-payout arrangement should become effective for the farmor. In any other situation, a dispute could arise as to whether the point has arisen when the farmor can benefit from the post-payout arrangement. This could lead to a consideration of the range of costs and expenses which might be recoverable by the farmee in counting towards the realisation of the payout point, which would be similar to the determination of deductible costs in relation to an NPI (B4).

A dispute could also arise where a farmout agreement says (in broad terms) that the payout point occurs when the revenues which have

"A dispute could also arise where a farmout agreement says (in broad terms) that the payout point occurs when the revenues which have been realised by the farmee from the production of petroleum equal the quantum of the associated costs and expenses which have been incurred by the farmee."

been realised by the farmee from the production of petroleum equal the quantum of the associated costs and expenses which have been incurred by the farmee. This might sound simple enough, and the revenues which have been realised by the farmee should be readily quantifiable; but the farmee could apply an expansive definition of the associated costs and expenses (if they are not otherwise explicitly defined in the farmout agreement), so that it takes longer for the revenue side of the equation to catch up with the costs side and so that the payout point is thereby deferred.

E3 Volumetric production payments

A volumetric production payment (VPP) is a financing arrangement (which is commonly structured as a hybrid of a forward sale of petroleum and a loan arrangement) whereby a producer (sometimes otherwise called 'the issuer' or 'the seller') secures an upfront cash payment from an investor (sometimes otherwise called 'the holder' or 'the purchaser'). The producer could apply the proceeds of the VPP to meet costs and expenses which are due in relation to the concessionary interests, or to repay other debt or costs commitments which the producer has.

Repayment of the cash payment by the producer to the investor is secured through the investor's right to receive a specific share (in kind) of the petroleum which is produced under the concessionary interests.[57] The investor will then sell its in-kind petroleum entitlements to realise a cash value (or the investor's entitlements could be marketed and sold by the producer on the investor's behalf).

Structurally, this would appear as follows:

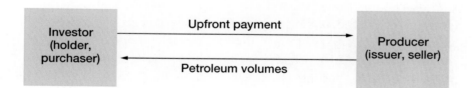

A VPP monetises the producer's interests through the conversion of unproduced in-ground petroleum resources into capital for the producer (which also generates in-kind petroleum quantities and the resulting cash flow for the investor), but without affecting the producer's ownership of the concessionary interests.

The VPP will have a limited term, and will be set to expire after a defined quantity of petroleum has been delivered by the producer to the investor in satisfaction of the investor's investment. The characterisation of the VPP as a loan arrangement could allow the producer to mark an element of the investor's petroleum entitlements as an interest payment, and so as tax deductible. The investor takes no part in the producer's petroleum production activities and has no exposure to the associated production expenses. On the other hand, the investor bears reserves risk in respect of:

- the concessionary interests (and so will likely carry out certain due diligence before making the investment);
- petroleum price risks (and so could hedge its petroleum entitlements); and
- ongoing operational risk in respect of the producer (and the producer's coventurers).

A VPP could contain several elements which appear to be similar to the content of a royalty interest.[58] An essential difference to note, however, is that under a VPP, a failure of the producer to deliver a quantity of petroleum to the investor when due would be an event of default (with the requirement that the shortfall must be made good by the producer, with accumulated interest). In contrast, a royalty interest will not ordinarily define a quota-based quantity of petroleum which is due for periodic delivery by the producer, where the producer's failure to make such delivery would be regarded as a breach of contract.

E4 Illustrative agreement participation

Under what is sometimes called an 'illustrative agreement', a person which is not party to a set of concessionary interests agrees to fund a share of the costs of petroleum production which would otherwise be due for payment by a person which is party to the concessionary interests. This funding commitment applies typically on a going-forward basis, rather than as an upfront payment, as could be the case where a royalty interest is used as a vehicle for financial investment (A3.1). In return, the funding person is entitled to take a corresponding share of the proceeds which accrue from the sale of petroleum (net of the associated costs of production), but without the funding person actually becoming party to the concessionary interests.

This arrangement could apply in respect of the nominated beneficiary of a participation (back-in) right which the grantor of a concession holds, where the existing parties to the concessionary interests do not wish to admit that nominee as a voting and paying member of the JOA consortium. In this circumstance the nominee would abide by the JOA operator's determination of revenues and costs, and would essentially be the holder of a net profit interest (B4).

Because the funding person is not party to the JOA, there is no mechanism by which the operator can cash call that person for the payments which it is required to make or to enforce a payment failure by that person through using the JOA's default provisions. The operator could therefore pay the amounts which are due for payment by that person and could offset those amounts against the share of the proceeds which accrue from the sale of petroleum which are due to that person. This is similar to the concept of the running account which was suggested in relation to an NPI (D12).

Notes

1 Sometimes otherwise called an 'overriding interest' or an 'overriding royalty', which can be confused with the description of a 'gross overriding royalty' which follows in this Special Report. See also footnotes 4 and 58. The terminology in this area is imprecise and it is often applied inconsistently.

2 Sometimes otherwise called a 'royalty payor'.

3 Sometimes otherwise called a 'royalty owner'.

4 A partial exception to this observation comes from Canada, where in 2015 the Canadian Association of Petroleum Landmen (CAPL) published the second edition of what it calls the 'overriding royalty procedure'. This is a *pro forma* royalty agreement for use in Canada, which is tied closely to the 2015 CAPL Operating Procedure (the standard Canadian JOA and assumes the creation of a royalty interest as a real property interest. The overriding royalty procedure creates what it calls the 'overriding royalty' as a royalty in kind for the royalty holder (with provision for the producer to sell the royalty holder's entitlements as agent or to purchase them for its own account), and with optional provisions for the royalty holder to be responsible for a share of certain of the associated costs of production.

5 See Section 30 of the Petroleum Act 1998 in the United Kingdom. This provision states that the list of persons which could be obliged to submit an abandonment programme in respect of an offshore petroleum installation could include "a person ... who is a party to a joint operating agreement or similar agreement relating to rights" and "a person ... who owns any interest in the installation otherwise than as security for a loan". Being a royalty holder does not per se expose a person to this legislation, but this is not a situation which a royalty holder should wish to debate the uncertainty of.

6 See the IPIECA Petroleum Industry Guidelines for Reporting Greenhouse Gas Emissions (2nd edition, May 2011, www.ipieca.org/resources/good-practice/petroleum-industry-guidelines-for-reporting-greenhouse-gas-emissions-2nd-edition/).

7 Where the amounts which are payable to the investor under the royalty interest are sometimes called a 'stream' and the investor is sometimes called a 'royalty company'.

8 The terms of the royalty interest could be made an inherent part of a wider financing agreement, rather than the royalty interest being represented in a standalone royalty agreement. This is imprudent, because if in the future there is a need to consider the disclosure (C3.1) or the transfer (C13) or the registration (D10) of the royalty interest, then the commercially sensitive terms of the wider financing arrangement could also be disclosed.

9 For the same reasons indicated in footnote 8, the royalty interest should be recited in a standalone royalty agreement rather than be embedded within the terms of a wider sale and purchase agreement or farmout agreement.

10 The US royalty model represents something of a combination of the transfer of interest and the provision of development finance models which are referred to above.

11 See John Burritt McArthur, *Oil and Gas Implied Covenants for the 21st Century* (Juris Publishing Inc, 2014).

12 "The centrality of securing revenue from production, with the lessor's accompanying right to royalty payments, is the fundamental driver of implied covenant litigation" (*ibid*, p27).

13 To give this some physical context, the wellhead is the surface termination point of a petroleum producing wellbore at which the flow of petroleum can be controlled. The problems which could result from defining the ambit of a royalty interest where there are multiple production wellheads in respect of a particular upstream petroleum granting interest should be addressed in the royalty agreement.

14 In a manner similar to the seller's reservations under a gas sale and purchase agreement relating, for example, to the seller's use of gas as fuel or for gas lift and the rights of the seller to flare, commingle and process gas prior to delivery, all in the ordinary course of business.

15 This exclusion from what is included as produced petroleum covers the application of the default mechanism under the JOA, where the producer is a non-defaulting party and has sequestrated the petroleum lifting entitlements of one of its coventurers which is a defaulting party. These sequestered petroleum quantities should not be included as part of the producer's lifting entitlement from which the royalty holder's royalty interest is calculated, but this is not always made clear in a royalty agreement. On the other hand, if the producer is a defaulting party and its coventurers sequestrate its petroleum lifting entitlements, then the intended application of the royalty interest will be neutralised. The royalty agreement could recognise this point explicitly, so that an event of default by the producer in respect of the royalty agreement (C7) would not occur in this circumstance.

16 But note also the possibility of the producer being subject to a production covenant in respect of its participation in exclusive operations (C8).

17 Sometimes called the producer's 'net working interest'.

18 Additionally, some upstream petroleum granting instruments will recite a percentage interest share of the producer as a holder of the instrument. The percentage interest shares should be the same across the upstream petroleum granting instrument and the JOA.

19 As an example of this 'Producers 88', which is a widely used lease and royalty agreement in the United States, applies the following royalty formulation:

As royalty, lessee covenants and agrees: (a) to deliver to the credit of lessor, in the pipe line to which lessee may connect its wells, the equal one-eighth part of all oil produced and saved by lessee from said land, or from time to time, at the options of lessee, to pay lessor the average posted market price of such one-eighth part of such oil at the wells as of the day it is run to the pipe line or storage tanks, lessor's interest, in either case, to bear of the cost of treating oil to render it marketable pipe line oil; (b) To pay lessor on gas and casinghead gas produced from said land (1) when sold by lessee, one-eighth of the amount realized by lessee, computed at the mouth of the well, or (2) when used by lessee off said land or in the manufacture of gasoline or other products, the market value, at the mouth of the well, of one-eighth of such gas and casinghead gas.

20 Although this arrangement would appear to be similar to a cash royalty from the royalty holder's perspective, the essential distinction to note is that the royalty holder could at any time end the sales agency arrangement with the producer and could thereafter assume responsibility itself for the commercialisation of its in-kind petroleum quantities. The same result could be achieved by the royalty holder having a right under the royalty agreement to elect to receive a royalty in kind or a cash royalty (see above).

21 Sometimes otherwise called an 'overriding royalty interest'.

22 Sometimes otherwise called a 'net revenue interest'.

23 Debating the virtues of the economic characteristics which are possessed by each of the GOR and the NPI is reminiscent of the debate which exists in the design of upstream petroleum granting instruments as to which of a production sharing contract (with priority cost recovery from gross revenues for the contractor before the division of profits is effected between the parties) and a revenue sharing contract (which divides revenues between the parties without first allocating the incidence of the costs) represents the best economic position.

24 In theory, this might also expose the royalty holder to the risk of a negative royalty and an obligation to make payment to the producer, for which a running account of revenues and costs could be a solution (D12).

25 Where the underlying upstream petroleum granting instrument is a production sharing contract (A4) which contains a definition of costs which are recoverable by the contractor for cost recovery purposes, an option to consider is the application of that definition to determine the deductible costs under the NPI. This could open the door to an argument about the double recovery of costs by the producer, however (see below).

26 This process is sometimes described as 'netback to wellhead', reflective of the incidence of costs which arise after petroleum has been produced at the wellhead.

27 It follows, therefore, that where the producer sells petroleum to a buyer at the wellhead, without the incidence of these various subsequent processing and handling costs and with the buyer assuming responsibility for the costs of compression, transportation and storage of the petroleum after delivery at the wellhead, there will be no post-production costs to be allocated between the producer and the royalty holder under the NPI.

28 In this instance the royalty agreement could also describe the royalty interest as an 'incorporeal interest'. This is intended to recognise the royalty interest as an enforceable real property interest, but also as a right which is intangible in that it cannot be possessed physically by the holder of the interest.

29 Some royalty agreements are worded to say that the royalty interest is 'carved out' of the upstream petroleum granting instrument.

30 One potential advantage of creating the royalty interest as a conveyable real property interest (wherever that is a possibility) is that the royalty holder's prospective petroleum entitlements would not form part of the producer's estate in the event of the producer's insolvency.

31 Notably Australia, Canada and most states of the United States. Even in these jurisdictions, the question of whether a royalty interest creates a real property interest in all cases tends to generate some differences of opinion. These jurisdictions also have their own rules as to how a royalty interest should be registered, and the extent to which registration of such an interest as an encumbrance over a property interest will afford priority of recovery against other registrants in the event of foreclosure.

32 Noting also that an identified third party which has the benefit of a permitted encumbrance (D7) over a royalty interest, or which is a beneficiary of a subdivision of the royalty interest (C13), could be the beneficiary of rights which legislation such as the Contract (Rights of Third Parties) Act 1999 in the United Kingdom seeks to address.

33 A royalty agreement could seek to give the royalty holder a right to take over (for its own account) the continued production of petroleum from an upstream petroleum granting instrument which the producer is prepared to surrender, or from production wells and facilities which the producer is prepared to decommission. Such a right would be difficult to exercise in practical terms where the royalty holder is not already a party to the concessionary interests; and even then, the exercise of such a right would have to effected in a manner which is consistent with the terms of the concessionary interests.

34 Broadly, such a rule is intended to ensure that a future property interest must vest within a defined period of time (known as the perpetuity period), in the interests of avoiding the sterilising effect of long-lasting contingencies. An arrangement which offends the rule against perpetuities could be declared void.

35 Under English law, the Perpetuities and Accumulations Act 2009 provides that an interest to which the Act applies must vest within a statutory period of 125 years from the date of the interest's creation.

36 Under English law it is necessary to identify "a settled trade custom in the sense of an invariable, certain and notorious usage, such as could imply a term into a contract" (*Thomas Crema v Cenkos Securities Plc* [2011] EWCA Civ 1444, per Aiken LJ).

37 "It has been common practice...to hear evidence of market practice, which does not amount to evidence of an alleged trade usage or custom" (*Thomas Crema v Cenkos Securities Plc, ibid*, per Aiken LJ).

38 In either case, this would be a breach of the royalty agreement only if the agreement contained a positive obligation of the producer to produce and to sell petroleum (C8).

39 *Cavendish Square Holding BV v Talal El Makdessi, Parking Eye Limited v Beavis* [2015] UKSC 67.

40 The producer will not be subject to an implied obligation to develop the production of petroleum, although it could have an obvious commercial incentive to do so, and so this should be made explicit.

41 Including, in respect of an NPI, a possible covenant that the producer will not become party to any arrangements for the sale or supply of petroleum for which it will receive no, reduced or deferred payment for delivered quantities.

42 A process which is sometimes referred to as 'stapling'.

43 The CAPL overriding royalty procedure (A2) creates a lien and charge (as a real property encumbrance) over the producer's working interests as security for amounts which are due for payment by the producer to the royalty holder.

44 See also the back-in after payout arrangement (E2) for an example of a conversion right.

45 It will also be necessary to ensure that the percentage part of the producer's interests under the concessionary interests which would be transferred to the royalty holder is not less than the minimum level of percentage interests which the JOA typically states which a person must have in order to be constituted as a party to the JOA.

46 "The phrase 'fiduciary duties' is a dangerous one, giving rise to a mistaken assumption that all fiduciaries owe the same duties in all circumstances. That is not the case" (per Lord Herschell, *Bray v Ford* [1896] AC44).

47 The • % factor component is a discount factor, intended to reflect the benefit to the royalty holder of an accelerated receipt of its expectations under the royalty agreement.

48 Alternatively, the previous payment amount could be averaged over a number of years to give a longer and perhaps more representative payment profile.

49 A royalty interest is not the sole occupant of the twilight world of arrangements which could potentially be registrable as a public declaration of existence and intended endurance. Other similar creatures include area of mutual interest agreements, carried interests, forward petroleum purchases, joint study and bid agreements, participation rights and unregistered charges and mortgages.

50 Such a provision is sometimes known as an 'anti-washout' provision.

51 A time condition will limit the application of this provision to a replacement upstream petroleum granting instrument which comes into existence within a relatively short period after the end of the original upstream petroleum granting instrument and prevents the potential for confusion which could result from the attempted application of this provision many years later. Alternatively, the royalty holder's rights could be expressed to apply at any later time when a replacement upstream petroleum granting instrument comes into existence in relation to the producer (sometimes described as a 'revival' provision). Care will need to be taken to ensure that long-term future arrangements do not offend a rule against perpetuities (C4.2).

52 Despite becoming coventurers in the development of the concessionary interests, it is not common for a bespoke JOA to be put in place between the farmor and the farmee to reflect the creation of their relationship as such. Rather, the key principles of their cooperation will be recited in the farmout agreement.

53 The point made in footnote 52 will apply equally.

54 Sometimes otherwise called the 'return on investment date'.

55 An alternative formulation which sometimes appears says that the farmee has no obligation to make any payments to the farmor under the royalty interest until the payout point is reached. Only then would the farmee's obligation to make royalty payments commence (and for this reason this formulation is sometimes described as a 'royalty holiday').

56 Through, for example, the inclusion of a clear statement of the costs and expenses which were incurred by the farmee which can be counted towards determining the payout point, possibly also with numerical values.

57 In the United States, a VPP is treated as the conveyance of a real property interest by the producer.

58 In some VPP arrangements, the petroleum entitlements which are identified as due for delivery to the investor over the term of the VPP are described as creating an 'overriding royalty interest'.

About the author

Peter Roberts
Principal, Cross Keys Energy
petro@crosskeysenergy.com

Peter Roberts is the principal of Cross Keys Energy, an independent energy consultancy. He is an oil and gas projects lawyer with 30 years of legal and commercial experience working for oil and gas companies on acquiring, structuring, developing and financing upstream, midstream and downstream petroleum projects, and also for governments on oil and gas sector regulatory matters.

He was worked extensively in Asia, Africa, Central and Eastern Europe and South America, and has previously worked in-house and as a partner in several international law firms. He also appears as an expert witness in energy sector disputes.

He is the author of several leading energy sector textbooks; is an honorary lecturer at Dundee University and a visiting professor of law at Austral University in Buenos Aires; and is the editor of the Association of International Petroleum Negotiators' *Journal of World Energy Law and Business*.

About Globe Law and Business

Globe Law and Business was established in 2005. From the very beginning, we set out to create law books which are sufficiently high level to be of real use to the experienced professional, yet still accessible and easy to navigate. Most of our authors are drawn from Magic Circle and other top commercial firms, both in the UK and internationally.

Our titles are carefully produced, with the utmost attention paid to editorial, design and production processes. We hope this results in high-quality publications that are easy to read, and a pleasure to own. Our titles are also available as ebooks, which are compatible with most desktop, laptop and tablet devices. In 2018 we expanded our portfolio to include journals and Special Reports, available both digitally and in hard copy format, and produced to the same high standards as our books.

In the Spring of 2021, we were very pleased to announce the start of a new chapter for Globe Law and Business following the acquisition of law books under the imprint Ark Publishing. We are very much looking forward to working with our new Ark authors, many of whom are well-known to us, and to further developing the law firm management list, among other areas.

We'd very much like to hear from you with your thoughts and ideas for improving what we offer. Please do feel free to email me at sian@globelawandbusiness.com with your views.

Sian O'Neill
Managing director
Globe Law and Business
www.globelawandbusiness.com